MESSAGE OF
SHRI SAI

MESSAGE OF
SHRI SAI

Suresh Chandra Panda

STERLING

STERLING PAPERBACKS
An imprint of
Sterling Publishers (P) Ltd.
Regd. Office: A-59, Okhla Industrial Area, Phase-II,
New Delhi-110020. CIN: U22110PB1964PTC002569
Tel: 26387070, 26386209; Fax: 91-11-26383788
E-mail: mail@sterlingpublishers.com
www.sterlingpublishers.com

Originally written in Odia by Suresh Chandra Panda
English Translation by Smita Panda
Message of Shri Sai
© 2015, Suresh Chandra Panda
ISBN 978 81 207 9512 9

Printed in India

Printed and Published by Sterling Publishers Pvt. Ltd.,
New Delhi-110020.

Dedicated to my beloved mother

Late Kamala Devi

*who has been a pillar of strength and support in my life
as well as in my spiritual pursuit*

Dr. C. B. Satpathy

Foreword

I had the pleasure of going through the manuscript of this book, *Message of Shri Sai*, written by Shri Suresh Chandra Panda. Shri Panda, a senior officer of the Indian Administrative Service, has also written a book titled *Shirdi Sai Baba – The Perfect Master*, co-authored with his wife, Mrs Smita Panda. He is an ardent devotee of Shri Shirdi Sai Baba since the last two decades.

This book contains articles on the preaching and divine activities of Shri Shirdi Sai Baba during His earthly sojourn. A close study will indicate that Baba practised and prophesized rendering service in two ways – *Service to God* and *Service to Mankind*. Further analysis will show that He practised and propagated the theme of service not only towards the human race, but also to other species as well. For some of His devotees He was an incarnation, for some He was a Sadguru, and for many others He was a father figure. He cared much for His devotees and reared them with filial love.

Through this book, the author attempts to present some of the divine attributes of Baba like humility, compassion, forgiveness, selfless service, dispassion, and benevolence. This book also brings to fore the other aspects of His personality like His moods of divine ecstasy, control and utilization of Yogic powers for individual and social good, and His divine knowledge of spiritual and religious issues. His divine majesty and spiritual magnificence endear Him to all that happen to come into His contact. Truly, He was the *Qutab* (a pivot around which things rotate) around which the pulsating life of Shirdi revolved. In the life of the devotees, He was the beginning and the end.

The intention of the author in writing this book becomes clear while reading it. He, in a subtle manner, sends a message to the readers to imbibe the qualities of a Sadguru. A study of this book will help the devotees to harmonize with the thought process and idealisms of Shri Sai. The readers will be immensely benefitted if they go through this book with the sincerity it deserves. May I expect the author, Shri Panda, to endeavour to write more books on such topics.

May Shri Sai bless the author and the readers of this work.

New Delhi   **C. B. Satpathy**

Preface

This book was originally written in Odia under the title *Sai Sandesh* and has seen three editions. It has a very humble beginning. With the inspiration of Guruji Shri Chandra Bhanu Satpathy, it was decided to build a temple of Shri Shirdi Sai Baba at Bhubaneswar. Further, Guruji cherished a noble thought. He was of the view that prior to the commencement of construction of the Sai Temple, the message of Sai should be spread among the people of the capital city of Bhubaneswar and, for that matter, the entire State of Odisha. This was more important than the building of the temple itself. Hence, the ideals and message of Sai Baba should be spread through print media, bhajans, and satsang.

As luck would have it, a small, beautiful statue of Shri Shirdi Sai came from Mumbai, gifted by a Sai devotee, Shri Amiya Kumar Sahu. I was moved by the speed with which things were happening. The construction work had not even commenced and Baba had arrived! I consulted with Guruji. Guruji made it very clear that Baba's statue should be kept in our house and worshipped daily while the temple was being constructed.

So the Sai movement, as desired and envisioned by Guruji, started. Daily worship of Baba began at our house at Palashpalli, Bhubaneswar. Every Thursday bhajan was conducted there with many people from nearby areas coming to attend it. A quarterly magazine, *Sai Bani*, in Odia, was started with a view to create awareness about the life and ideals of Sai Baba. I contributed articles on Shirdi Sai Baba and His message to mankind in several Odia newspapers

(*The Samaj, Dharitree, and Pragatibadi*) quite regularly. As the articles were very popular among Sai devotees, there were requests from friends and well-wishers to compile them and publish them in the form of a book. So the Odia book, *Sai Sandesh*, with all these articles, was published in the year 1998. And now, by Baba's grace, this book, which is its English version, has also arrived due to the dedicated effort of my dear wife Smita in translating it into English.

Sai Baba never used to give any *mantradiksha* or sermons to the people. He has said a number of times that *Mein koi Kaanphukana Guru nahin*, meaning "I am not a Guru (Master) who gives any mantra in your ear." He used to have a durbar in His dilapidated masjid, fondly called Dwarkamayi, with His devotees and visitors. He used to talk to them, listen to their mundane problems, share jokes with them, and gave them assurance and solace. He used to go for begging to Shirdi village and partake whatever He used to get as offering, along with His dear devotees and followers. He would sometimes accept dakshina (monetary offering) from some devotees and except for using a small amount of the dakshina for purchasing tobacco for His chillum and fuel for the ever-burning dhuni, He would donate the rest of the amount among poor people, musicians, and the needy devotees.

His life was His message. His simple talks with devotees and followers, His gestures and instructions, had more universal message than any instruction or *mantradiksha*. Though in the initial days of His stay at Shirdi, He was regarded as a mad fakir, slowly and gradually more and more people started visiting Him and towards the last part of His bodily sojourn at Shirdi, hundreds of devotees used to come to Shirdi to see their beloved Master, Sai.

Baba has said to some of His dear devotees that a large number of people will come to this place (Shirdi) like ants forming a long line and it will dazzle with lights and other modern amenities. Many could not believe this in those days because Shirdi was a village with forty–fifty houses and without any signs of a town life. But those of us who have been to Shirdi in the recent past would have seen the large crowds of visitors on any day, the large number of hotels, restaurants and other amenities for the surging crowd, and the tall and brightly lit buildings.

I hope this humble contribution from both my wife and I will help to spread the universal message of Sai, which has an appeal for people of all ages, all religions, and creeds, all over the world. Ultimately, the real happiness lies in understanding, assimilating, and following the ideals of Sai Baba.

Jai Shri Sai!

Suresh Chandra Panda

Contents

1

Doership and Discharge
of Duty

In the old Nizam State, there was a dear devotee of Sai Baba named Pundalikrao, who resided in the city of Nanded. Once he had gone to South to meet Tembe Swami (Swami Vasudevananda Saraswati) who had his ashram on the banks of river Godavari. On meeting Tembe Swami, Pundalikrao paid his obeisance and started a conversation. During the discussion, the name of Sai Baba of Shirdi cropped up. Tembe Swami closed his eyes for a moment and then said, "Please convey my utmost regards to my elder brother Sai Baba." Then he went inside his ashram, brought a coconut and requested Pundalikrao to give it to Sai Baba when he reached Shirdi. Pundalikrao promised to convey his regards to Baba, as well as hand over the coconut to Him. Then he took leave and started his journey to Shirdi.

After some time, Pundalikrao and his group reached Manmad. They were all very thirsty and wanted to quench their thirst by drinking water. However, since water should not be drunk on an empty stomach, they wanted to eat something. There was *chivda* (flattened rice) and, to make it palatable, one of the members of the group broke the coconut that Tembe Swami had given to Pundalikrao, and mixed it with the chivda. This was served to everyone.

When Pundalikrao came to know that the coconut meant for Baba was consumed, he felt very disturbed and was extremely upset. After reaching Shirdi, he kept his luggage at the wada (resting place or guesthouse) and went for Baba's darshan. Baba, in the meantime had already received a telepathic message regarding the coconut and asked Pundalikrao, *"Where is the coconut which was sent by my brother, Tembe Swami?"* With a sense of guilt and negligence, he asked for His forgiveness. He offered to give another coconut as a substitute, but Baba refused to accept it, saying that the worth of the coconut given by His brother Tembe Swami was far more than any other coconut and so could not be substituted. Then Baba told Pundalikrao in a reprimanding tone, *"If you undertake any responsibility, carry it out with utmost sincerity; otherwise don't take the responsibility at all."*

Pundalikrao, with all humility and repentance, touched Baba's feet and asked for Baba's pardon. Sai Baba then spoke in a softer tone, *"Now you need not worry yourself any more about the matter, since before eating the coconut, you have offered it to Me, it was accepted by Me also."*

Baba then added, *"Why should you take the responsibility of your actions? Do not entertain the sense of doership for doing good as well as for any bad deed; be entirely prideless and egoless and this will hasten your spiritual progress."*

What a perfect spiritual instruction Baba has imparted, which should be followed by every true devotee of Baba!

*****

Self Restraint

Nanasaheb Chandorkar was a dear devotee of Sai Baba. At that time, he was a highly placed revenue official in Ahmednagar district. In spite of his position and rank, he was a humble and true devotee of Baba.

Once Nanasaheb was attending the darbar of Baba, along with Mahlsapati and others, in Dwarkamayi masjid. The masjid was dilapidated and abandoned, but Baba had made it His abode and had fondly named it Dwarkamayi. Dwarkamayi welcomed people from all religions and sects with equal love. Nana was sitting beside Baba, as the flow of visitors to the darbar continued. Two veiled Muslim ladies were there among the visitors. They remained in the courtyard, waiting for others to leave so that they could take Baba's darshan in seclusion and privacy. Understanding the situation, Nana got up to leave the place. Baba, at that time, stopped Nana and made him sit down, saying, "*Those who want to meet me, let them come. You don't have to leave this place.*" Finally, the two veiled ladies came near Baba. Lifting their veils, they prostrated in front of Him. One of the ladies was elderly, but the other was young, extremely beautiful, and attractive. Nana, who had a brief glimpse of her face, was attracted by her beauty and he desired to see her face again.

Baba could perceive the restlessness of Nana's mind, as nothing was hidden from Him. Baba spoke to Nana after the ladies departed from the place, "*Nana, why are you getting agitated in vain?*" The *antaryami* Baba could know the mind of Nana. Nana felt abashed and said, "Although I was sitting in such close proximity to You, how could I entertain such impure thoughts in my mind?"

To answer this question, Baba spoke very softly, "*After all, you have taken human birth and this body is made up of flesh and blood with all the senses in action and doing their respective work. When the senses come in contact with an external object, they become active and alert. Let the senses do their allotted work or duty. We should not interfere with them. God has created this beautiful world and it is our duty to appreciate its beauty. The mind will get steady and calm gradually. When the heart is pure, there is no difficulty. Why should we be afraid of anything, if there is no evil thought in us? The eyes may do their work, why should you feel shy and awkward?*" Baba continued to explain, "*Don't we find temples with beautiful carvings and rich architecture? When we visit a temple, do we only enjoy and appreciate the beauty of the temple, or do we go inside for taking the darshan of the deity also? In a similar manner, try to see the Creator in any beautiful creature you behold. God is not confined only to temples. He resides in every living creature, He has created.*

When Baba was explaining, Shama, who was present there, could not follow the meaning of all that He had said. So, he asked Nana about it on their way home. Nana narrated the restlessness of his mind at the sight of the beautiful lady, how Baba came to know it, and how He advised accordingly.

The meaning of Baba's advice was explained by Nana to Shama as follows: "*Our mind is fickle by nature. However, we should not allow it to go astray. The senses may get restless, the body should, nonetheless, be held in restraint. Senses run after objects of desire, but we should not crave for them. By slow and gradual practice, we can conquer our restlessness of mind. Beauty* is a subject of sight; we may fearlessly look at the beauty of objects. However, we should never entertain evil thoughts. In this way, the senses can be brought under our control and when we enjoy an object, we will be reminded of its Creator, that is, God. Making the mind desireless, we can observe and appreciate God's works of beauty."

*****

Shradha and Saburi

Although, Baba lived a very simple and ordinary life, His greatness and generosity attracted a lot of devotees to Shirdi. His fame spread far beyond the boundaries of Maharashtra, to every nook and corner of India, towards the end of the nineteenth century. Many visitors and devotees flocked to Shirdi to receive the blessings of this great seer as well as to receive His spiritual guidance.

Radhabai Deshmukh, an elderly lady, heard the name and fame of Sai Baba and came to Shirdi, along with other devotees, for His darshan. After taking Baba's darshan, she was immensely satisfied. She started thinking that so far her life had been wasted, since she had not been able to meet such a great *Satpurush* earlier and felt remorseful. She immediately accepted Baba as her Guru and wanted to get some *mantra-diksha* (initiation) or upadesha from Him. When she bowed down before Baba, she expressed her keen desire in this regard. But Baba did not give any reply and kept quiet. This was because Sainath has never attached any importance to mantra or upadesha as a medium of attaining spiritual progress. Radhabai Deshmukh felt sad and dejected and left for the wada with a heavy heart. However, she took a firm resolution to fast unto death till Baba had blessed her by imparting some diksha to her.

After three days of fast, the old lady's condition started deteriorating and became critical. Shama, a dear devotee of

Baba, was frightened by this ordeal of the old woman and spoke to Baba on her behalf. He pleaded with Him to impart some upadesha or mantra to the old lady to bless and save her from impending death. Sai Baba summoned the old lady from the wada, made her sit next to Him and addressed her very lovingly, *"Oh mother, why do you have to subject yourself to unnecessary torture? You are My mother and I am your child, take pity on Me and listen carefully to what I have to say. I had a guru, who was a great saint and most merciful. I served My guru for twelve long years with complete devotion. He also brought Me up with love and care. He took care of My food and every other need. I had a keen desire to serve him all My life, as well as to receive some mantra (instructions) from him, but, in vain. He never imparted any mantra to me during My entire stay. So what kind of mantra can I give you?*

"My guru was love-incarnate. He used to shower all his love on Me. Indeed, I am blessed to have served him and remain under his tutelage and care for twelve years. In return, My guru asked for two paise as dakshina from Me. You may say that, as My guru was perfect, why should he ask for money and how could he be called desireless? The reply is that he never cared for coins. What had he to do with them? His two paise were shradha (firm faith) and saburi (patience or perseverance).I gave these two paise to him and he was pleased.

"Rare is a guru like my guru. When I looked at him, he seemed as if he was in deep meditation and then, We both were filled with bliss. Night and day, I gazed at him, with no thought of hunger or thirst. I used to serve him with love and devotion. My mind was always fixed on my guru. I meditated on him as he was my sole refuge. This nishtha is shradha and is one paisa of dakshina.

"Saburi (patience or perseverance) is the other paisa. I waited patiently and served my guru. This saburi will ferry you across the sea of mundane existence. Saburi removes all sins and afflictions, gets rid of calamities in various ways, and casts aside all fear and ultimately gives you success. Saburi is the gateway leading to all

virtues and is the best among all virtues. Shradha and saburi are like two loving twin sisters, inseparable from each other.

"*My guru used to protect me by his mere loving glances. Oh mother, My guru never taught me any mantra, then how shall I blow any mantra in your ears? Just remember that guru's tortoise-like loving glance gives us spiritual bliss.*

"*Do not try to get mantra or upadesha from anybody. Make Me the sole object of your thoughts and actions and you will undoubtedly attain paramartha (the spiritual goal of life). Look at Me wholeheartedly and I, in turn, shall look at you. Sitting in this masjid, I speak the truth, nothing but the truth. No sadhana or proficiency in the six Shastras is necessary. Have faith and confidence in your guru. Believe that guru is the sole doer. Blessed is he who knows the greatness of his guru and realizes him as Trimurti incarnate (the Holy Trinity — Lord Brahma, the creator; Lord Vishnu, the preserver; and Lord Shiva, the destroyer)."*

Instructed in this way, the old lady was convinced and gave up her fast. She remained a staunch devotee of Baba till her end.

*****

The Mystery of Dakshina

In Indian civilization, saints and seers have been traditionally assigned the titles of *Maharaj* and *Rajadhiraj*. But often it has been observed that great saints who are pious and pure in heart and deed have lived a very austere and unostentatious life, totally indifferent and detached from materialistic world. Sai Baba of Shirdi lived the life of a fakir (renunciant or mendicant). He lived in a dilapidated masjid in Shirdi. Begging alms from door to door in the village of Shirdi constituted an integral part of His daily life. He used to wear a long robe called *kafni* and tie his head with another long piece of cloth. This piece of cloth on the head was twisted like matted hair and flowed down from the left ear to the back. He wore neither shoes nor sandals. When He used to go on His begging rounds, He used to carry a tumrel (tin pot) and a *jholi* (cloth bag). The liquid food items, like vegetable soup and milk, would go into the tumrel and the dry food items like rotis and rice were kept in the jholi by Baba.

The only requirements of Baba used to be tobacco for His chillum (an earthen pipe) and firewood for his perpetually burning *dhuni* (sacred fire). By and by, Baba's greatness attracted one and all towards Him and the number of visitors and devotees visiting Shirdi for Baba's darshan started increasing. The visitors and devotees used to offer Him dakshina which, He would accept. A fakir like Baba accepting dakshina from His devotees was a mystery to many.

Most saints and seers consider money as an obstacle to spiritual progress and therefore look down upon it as an object of impurity and root cause of all evil. Ramakrishna Paramhansa used to tell his devotees to remain away from women and wealth as they were the two main obstacles in attaining paramartha. Baba also tested His devotees through dakshina. Whenever any devotee came to Him, He demanded dakshina from him. If the devotee stood the test well, that is, if he was free from attachment to wealth, his spiritual progress was assured by Baba's grace and blessings. Baba's demand for dakshina had significant spiritual undertones. Let us see some instances.

Once the Tarkhad couple (both were ardent devotees of Baba) visited Shirdi to take Baba's darshan. Baba asked Mrs Tarkhad to give ₹6 as dakshina. At that time, Mrs Tarkhad did not have any money. She felt pained and remorseful at her inadequacy and looked at her husband helplessly. Then, her husband came to her rescue and explained to her that, Baba wanted six inner enemies (lust, anger, avarice, greed, jealousy, and attachment) to be surrendered to Him. Baba agreed with this explanation.

In another similar incident, Baba asked for ₹15 as dakshina from Prof. G. G. Narke, who replied that he did not have even a pie. Then Baba said, "*I know you have no money, but you are reading Yoga Vasishtha. Give Me dakshina from it.*" Giving dakshina in this case meant to derive lessons from the book and lodge them in the heart, where Baba always resides.

Baba did not ask dakshina from all. If anyone gave dakshina unasked, He sometimes accepted and at other times refused it. This was because Baba's ways were inscrutable and beyond comprehension. Dakshina only manifested Baba's omniscience. Once Ratanji Shapurji Wadia, a Parsi businessman from Nanded, came to Shirdi for Baba's darshan. He was a prosperous person and used to do a lot of charity, but he did not have any children. He had come to Shirdi to seek Baba's blessings for a child. Sai Baba asked him ₹5 as dakshina, which Ratanji gladly wanted to give. Then Baba said, "*I have already received ₹3 and 14 annas. So pay Me the balance only.*" At that time, one rupee was equal to 16 annas. Hearing this, Ratanji was quite puzzled. He could not understand what Baba meant. Since he was visiting Shirdi for the first time, he wondered how he could have given Baba 3 rupees and 14 annas. Though he was unable to solve the riddle, he paid the balance amount to Baba with great humility and respect.

Later he remembered that, before coming to Shirdi, he had received a Mohammedan saint called Moulisaheb in his house and had spent exactly 3 rupees and 14 annas on him. This incident reveals the omniscience of Baba. Though Baba lived in Shirdi, He knew what happened outside, far away from Shirdi. In fact, He knew the past, present, and future and could identify Himself with anybody. In this particular instance, how could Baba know the reception given to Moulisaheb and the amount spent, unless He could identify Himself with Moulisaheb and be one with him?

Though Baba collected a lot of money in the form of dakshina, He would distribute the whole amount the same day itself and become a poor fakir by the evening, as usual. He would distribute *naivedya* and dakshina money among the poor and the needy, those who used to serve Baba (like cleaning the masjid, getting drinking water, etc.), and among musicians, kirtan groups, singers, etc. He only kept a small amount out of the dakshina in order to purchase tobacco for His chillum and fuel or firewood for His dhuni. According to Baba, "*Fakiri is kingship,*" which implies mendicancy is real and wealth is transient.

Whenever any person approaches a guru and aspires to become his devotee, or simply goes for darshan of saints and seers without any desires, he humbly offers some dakshina as a token of his reverence. Baba's main object in taking dakshina from His devotees was to teach them the lessons of renunciation and purification.

For several reasons, dakshina was a real and befitting test for the devotees. Firstly, it could be determined, among the several visitors, how many visited Shirdi with real devotion; whether the meanness and narrow mindedness like "this is mine" and "that is mine" had been eliminated from their mind or not could be tested through dakshina. Secondly, those who were attached to wealth and property would not come for darshan of Baba for fear of having to give dakshina to Him. So dakshina acted as a beautiful medium to test the detachment of an individual from materialism. Only those individuals who are prepared to pay dakshina or willing to lead a life of detachment by their true surrender can become disciples of a Sadguru.

Dakshina has another significant implication. When a Sadguru accepts dakshina from a devotee or a disciple, He frees him from his *rina* (debt) which has been accumulated due to his *prarabdha* (previous karmas).

Once, two gentlemen from Goa visited Shirdi to take Baba's darshan. Baba asked an amount of ₹15 as dakshina from one of them. The other gentleman voluntarily offered ₹35 as dakshina to Baba, which He refused instantly. At that time, Baba's dear devotee, Shama (Madhav Rao Deshpande), who was a witness to this incident, asked Baba, "What is this? Both came together; one's dakshina you accept, the other's, though voluntarily paid, you refuse. Why this distinction?" Baba replied, "*Shama, you know nothing. I take nothing from anybody. The Masjidmai (the presiding deity of the masjid) calls for the debt; the donor pays it and becomes free. I require nothing, I am ever free.*"

Then Baba explained the case of the two gentlemen. The first gentleman, from whom He accepted ₹15 as dakshina, hailed from a poor family. He had vowed to his *grihadevta* (family deity), Dattatreya, that he would pay his first month's salary, if he got a job. Subsequently, he got a job for a salary of ₹15 per month. Then he steadily got promotions. His salary increased from ₹15 to ₹30, ₹60, ₹100, ₹200 and, ultimately, to ₹700 per month. But in this period of rising prosperity, he had completely forgotten his vow to pay ₹15, his first month's salary. It was his good luck that he visited Dwarkamayi masjid, which redeemed his debt. Debt, enmity, and murder have to be atoned, as there is no escape from them. The second gentleman was an affluent person and when he offered ₹35 as dakshina to Baba, it was not accepted by Him. This was because the second gentleman had no debt to be got rid of and Baba never required any money or wealth.

In other words, Sai Baba accepted dakshina from his visitors and devotees as a medium to ascertain their detachment, to make them free from their debts, and for their spiritual upliftment. In this context, Upasani Maharaj, a dear devotee of Baba, has said, "In order to elevate yourself to a higher plane, if you have not given anything in charity, then saints and seers ask dakshina from you in order to grant something more precious in return." Sai Baba of Shirdi, Yaswant Rao Maharaj, Akalkot Swami—all used to take dakshina in the form of coins or some material possession, from their devotees. They were taking something ephemeral and, in return, were showering permanent spiritual bliss, which is priceless.

In the beginning of the twentieth century, around 1908–10, many visitors and devotees flocked to Shirdi, the abode of Baba. Around this time, there were some noticeable changes in the behaviour of Sai Baba in the form of increased usage of sign language or symbols. There is ample evidence that Baba gave instructions through sign language or symbols. Baba would give upadesha to some devotees by narrating stories and parables. He would choose some devotees and impart instructions for their spiritual upliftment. And sometimes it was observed that Baba would ask for dakshina from, what appeared to be, randomly selected devotees from the large gathering of visitors and devotees assembled in the masjid.

Once a devotee of Baba could not come to Shirdi for Baba's darshan as he was seriously ill. However, he sent some money as dakshina, to be given to Baba, through an acquaintance who was visiting Shirdi. As soon as Baba accepted the dakshina, He started shivering from fever. Here the dakshina was just a medium through which the illness of the devotee was taken over by Baba. The devotee, at the other end, recovered and became completely all right. This incident also reveals how Baba used to take upon himself the pain and illness of His devotees.

In many instances, Baba used dakshina as a symbolic gesture. Whenever Baba gave spiritual instructions to any devotee, He would ask for dakshina through sign language. Sai Baba, generally, used to ask two rupees as dakshina from most of His devotees. The actual meaning underlying was shradha and saburi. Baba often used to say in simple words, *"My guru asked from Me two rupees and I gave him."* By uttering these significant words, Baba used to inform His devotees that through shradha and saburi, one can receive *gurukripa* (blessings of guru), which will enable him to achieve all the chief objects of life, that is, *Dharma* (righteousness), *Artha* (wealth), *Kama* (desire), and *Moksha* (deliverance).

Sometimes, Baba used to ask for four rupees, as dakshina. Here, the number four refers to the mind, intelligence, conscience and ego, and Sai Baba's instruction was to surrender these attributes at the lotus feet of one's guru. In a similar manner, when Baba used to ask for six rupees as dakshina, the intention was the surrender of six inner enemies, that is, lust, anger, avarice, greed, jealousy, and attachment. In short, Baba's main object in taking dakshina from His devotees was to teach them the lessons of renunciation and purification.

Once a devotee offered a gold sovereign (coin) to Baba. However, he desired that Baba should consecrate the coin by His touch and return it to him so that he could keep it in his shrine. Omniscient Baba held the coin in his hand and tossed the coin. Then He asked the devotees who were sitting close by, *"What is this? I don't require it."* Returning the gold sovereign to its owner, Baba asked him to preserve it in his shrine and asked one rupee as dakshina from him. The significance of one rupee in this context was that Brahma is the only reality and the universe is ephemeral.

From the experience of devotees, it has been found that those who received coins from Baba were truly blessed and by preserving these consecrated coins in their shrines, their families were blessed with wealth and prosperity. Generally, acceptance of dakshina by Baba from His devotees was an indication of ensuring welfare and happiness.

*****

5

Baba's Incredible Methods of Cure

The spiritual history of our civilization has been a witness to the blessings of great saints and seers which has helped cure mankind of its afflictions, especially in treating those which had no cure. Sai Baba, the epitome of mercy and kindness, was always there for His devotees, ever caring and ever loving. His heart used to melt at their sufferings, to the extent that sometimes He would take upon Himself their sufferings. Day and night, He always thought and worked for their welfare. Innumerable devotees have been cured of their diseases by the unusual remedies during Baba's sojourn in Shirdi. He not only got rid of their pain and afflictions but also used to guide them in their spiritual journey.

It is very difficult to explain Baba's incredible methods of cure. Strange were Baba's methods of diagnosis of the disease and the remedies and medicines He would prescribe for their cure. There are many instances which show that the real thing that cured the diseases permanently was Baba's word and grace, and not any medicine or drug. The potency of Baba's word was absolute and whenever Baba placed His hand on a devotee's head, the devotee would feel immediate relief and there would be no further trouble arising from the malady.

Initially, Baba used to treat the village folk of Shirdi with His *jadi-buti* (herbs). Gradually, He stopped giving *jadi-buti* and instead gave *udi* (ash) from His sacred dhuni. It has been found that the udi cured many physical and mental illnesses. However, the greatness of udi is due to the spiritual attainment of Baba. Thousands of miles away from Shirdi, Baba's devotees used to get cured by application and oral intake of udi, as well as by sincerely and fervently praying to Baba. Baba's strange methods of cure were an enigma, even to some of His closest devotees.

The author of the original Marathi version of Shri Sai Satcharita, Annasaheb Dabholkar, who was fondly addressed as Hemadpant by Sai Baba, has observed a remarkable method of cure by Baba during His first visit to Shirdi. In the year 1910, Annasaheb visited Shirdi for the first time to take darshan of Baba, whose greatness he had heard from other devotees. At that time, Shirdi and its adjoining areas were inflicted with cholera. The village folks were extremely scared, to the extent that they even stopped moving in and out of the village boundaries. The result was that they even stopped getting their supplies of rations, vegetables, fuel, or wood from outside.

When Annasaheb went to the Dwarkamayi masjid for the first time to have Baba's darshan, he was astonished to behold a strange sight. There, in the masjid, Baba was busy grinding wheat in a hand mill. Immediately, the news of Baba's grinding wheat spread in Shirdi. Some bold women of Shirdi went up to Baba and forcibly took over the task of grinding the wheat. While they were grinding, they began to think that since Baba had no family and since He lived on alms, He had no requirement of the wheat flour. They thought that the kind hearted Baba would definitely distribute the flour among them. After finishing the task, they put aside the hand mill and divided the flour among themselves. Seeing this, Baba got angry and shouted at them, *"Ladies, have you gone mad? Have I borrowed any wheat from you that you are taking*

*away the flour? Now take this flour and throw it on the village
borders!"* On hearing this, the women felt abashed, went to
the outskirts of the village, and spread the flour along the
border as directed by Baba.

From that time onward, the cholera epidemic subsided
and the villagers of Shirdi felt very relieved. They believed
that it was not wheat but cholera which was ground to pieces
in Baba's hand mill and pushed out of the village. This was
a very unusual remedy of Baba. At that time, it was beyond
any spectator's comprehension what earthly connection there
was between wheat flour and cholera and what the causal
relation was between the two. The incident seemed simply
inexplicable. However, the truth was that Baba's pure grace
and blessings acted as a talisman, protecting them from all
evil forces.

Bapusaheb Buti was an affluent businessman from
Nagpur. Despite being a millionaire, he was a very humble
and dedicated devotee. He listened to Baba's advice with
complete humility and devotion. Once he suffered from
dysentery and started vomiting. He took several medicines
but all, in vain. On account of purgings and vomiting,
Bapusaheb became very weak and was unable to go to
Dwarkamayi for Baba's darshan. Baba, hearing about
Bapusaheb's helpless condition, summoned him. He made
him sit before Him and said, *"Be careful, you should not purge
any more. The vomiting must also stop."* Wonderful is the
potency of Baba's words! Both the maladies immediately
disappeared and Bapusaheb soon felt well.

On another occasion, Bapusaheb suffered from cholera.
Dr Pillai, another devotee of Baba, treated him with several
patented drugs. However, Bapusaheb's condition worsened
and the drugs could give him no relief. Then he approached
Baba and prayed to Him to cure him. Baba asked him to drink
milk with sugar and a lot of dry fruits like walnuts, almonds,
pistachios added to it. Any doctor or physician would have

been surprised at this remedy. However, a devout bhakta (devotee) like Buti took the milk in complete obedience to Baba's order and was cured.

The real reason behind the remedy was Baba's words and blessings. This is the experience of Buti and several other devotees. The devotees felt that Baba's loving and sympathetic glance, His soothing and nectar-like words and divine blessings were the factors in curing the various afflictions of His devotees.

*****

6

Greatness of Udi

The udi or the ash from the perpetually burning dhuni in the Dwarkamayi masjid is an integral and significant part of Baba's divinity. When Baba was resting in Dwarkamayi, He always sat in front of the dhuni, facing south. In the dhuni, He offered an oblation of egoism and desires and always said *"Allah Malik hai,"* implying that God is the sole owner. Sitting before the dhuni, Baba used to impart spiritual instructions to His devotees and would distribute udi as *prasad* among the visitors and devotees present in the masjid. All the visitors and devotees used to take udi prasad, as Baba's blessings, before their departure.

There is an inseparable link between Baba's daily routine life in Shirdi and udi. In reality, udi constituted the essence of all Sai leelas (miracles) and represented the benevolence of Shri Sainath. When the visitors and devotees used to take Baba's permission to depart from Shirdi, Baba would take out a fistful of warm udi from the dhuni and give it as prasad and besmear some of it on their foreheads. Those devotees, who were afflicted with sorrow and pain, were advised by Baba to take the udi by dissolving it in water and drinking it. As a result, they would get rid of their pain and afflictions and lead a healthy and carefree life. When Baba was in a cheerful mood, He used to sing merrily. One of the songs was about udi. The meaning of the song was, *"Oh playful Ram, come, come and bring with you sacks of udi."* The scene of Baba singing was spellbinding and heart moving.

In the initial days, Baba used to give *jadi-buti* to treat the villagers of Shirdi when they fell sick. But later on, Baba only gave udi as the remedy for all kinds of problems, be it physical or psychological. In the words of Baba, *"Udi is the remedy for all diseases and all pains."* Udi conferred health, prosperity, freedom from anxiety, and provided many other benefits. Many instances have been cited in Shri Sai Satcharita to prove that udi is the infallible remedy.

In Malegaon, a district of Nasik, there lived a highly qualified doctor. His nephew was suffering from tubercular bone abscess. The doctor, along with his medical team, tried all sorts of remedies and even surgery, but could not cure the boy. Then friends and relatives advised the parents of the boy to seek divine blessings and recommended them to visit Shirdi and take Baba's darshan.

Accepting Baba as the ultimate refuge, the parents visited Shirdi, along with their son. They went to Dwarkamayi and prostrated before Baba. Placing the boy before Him, both implored Him to save their son. The merciful Baba comforted them, saying, *"Those who resort to this masjid, shall never suffer anything in life. Apply udi on the abscess and within a week he will recover. Believe in God! This is no masjid, but Dwarkamayi. He who steps here, will soon get health and happiness, and his sufferings will come to an end."* Then Baba, very lovingly, stroked the affected part of the boy's body with His hands. With the application of udi, the boy began to recover and became completely well after a few days. The parents were extremely grateful to Baba for curing their son.

Another similar incident illustrates the significance of udi. Shama was a very dear devotee of Baba. His younger brother, Bapaji, was staying in a nearby village. Once Bapaji's wife was afflicted with bubonic plague. She suffered from high fever and two buboes developed in her groins, causing great pain. Bapaji rushed to his elder brother, Shama, at Shirdi and implored him to approach Baba and invoke His aid. Shama went to the masjid, prostrated before Baba and pleaded Him to cure his sister-in-law. He also sought Baba's permission to visit her. In response, Baba said, *"Do not go there at this late hour, send her the udi. Why care for the fever and buboes? Instead, visit her tomorrow morning and return immediately."*

Shama had full faith in Baba's udi. He sent it with Bapaji. The udi was applied on the buboes and some of it was mixed with water and given to the patient to drink. Immediately, the patient started perspiring profusely. The fever abated and the patient could sleep soundly. Next morning, Bapaji was surprised to find his wife well with no signs of either fever or buboes. When Shama reached their house later, he was also surprised to see her well and busy preparing tea in the kitchen. He found from his brother that Baba's udi had cured his sister-in-law overnight. Then Shama realized the significance of Baba's words, *"Go there in the morning and return immediately."*

But udi's greatness is not confined to curing dreadful and grave diseases only. This was only one aspect of udi, that is, material significance, which helped in gaining material ends. The spiritual significance of udi, which is the other aspect, has been clearly shown by Baba. Through udi, Baba taught that all the visible phenomena in the universe are as transient as the ash. Our body, which is composed of five elements, shall ultimately be reduced to ash. This is why Baba distributed udi to one and all, in order to remind them of this universal truth. Baba also taught by udi that Brahma is the only reality; the universe is ephemeral and no one in this world belongs to us—be it a son, a daughter, a father, a mother, a wife, or a husband. We have come alone to this world and will depart alone. Through udi, Baba has taught a very important principle of differentiating between the unreal and the real.

There are several incidents in man's life which cannot be easily erased from his mind. Among these unforgettable incidents, some are rare and divinely-ordained. Two real-life incidents may be narrated which are touching and incredible. They confirm the fact that udi is the ultimate cure for all kinds of afflictions. There is no attempt to exaggerate these incidents.

The first incident happened in June 1997. I had gone to Delhi on an official visit and was putting up in Odisha Niwas. Since the work took longer than envisaged, I had to extend my stay by another three days. It was a Sunday and after lunch I walked up to Odisha Bhawan, which was located across the road. At that time a white Ambassador car halted suddenly, in front of me. From the car alighted Smt. Indira Mahapatra, her husband, their son, and their daughter. They hail from Bhubaneswar. Indira is like a sister to me, as her paternal house is in Bapujinagar, next to our house.

On enquiring about their welfare, I came to know that their daughter, aged 13 years, was suffering from stones in her kidney and was undergoing treatment at the premier hospital, AIIMS. According to the X-ray reports, of the two stones found in her kidney, one had been removed through surgery. The doctors were contemplating a second surgery to remove the other stone. They had already been staying in Delhi for more than a fortnight and if the second surgery was to take place, their stay in Delhi would have to be extended. The entire family was undergoing a harrowing time. I looked at the young girl. Although, she was very beautiful with a fair complexion, she looked very pale and was in acute pain.

I took out Baba's photograph from my pocket, showed it to the girl and asked, "Do you recognize Baba?" She answered, "No," in a very feeble tone. I gave her the photo and asked her to think of Baba with love and devotion in the morning and at night before going to bed. I also took out a packet of udi, gave her some as prasad, and asked her to take a little udi with water every night before going to bed. Comforting the parents, I advised them not to go for the second surgery as the girl was not in a proper mental condition. I also added, "If Baba desires, the other stone may simply dissolve and no surgery would be required." I don't know from where these words came to my mouth—it seems they were uttered not by me but by someone else.

After two days, when the family visited the doctor for consultation, another X-ray was taken and, wonder of wonders, the report did not show the presence of any stone in the kidney! The doctors present there were amazed. How could this happen? But the girl had an answer.

The day she had taken Baba's udi from me, that night, the girl had felt some pain while easing herself in the restroom. Probably, the stone had dissolved and passed out of the body with the urine. After that, there was no pain. Clasping the photograph of Sai Baba closely to her chest, she was found crying with joy and bowing down to Baba, again and again. Indeed, wonderful is the power of udi!

Another incident happened in the year 2000. It was the eve of Deepawali and I was returning to Bhubaneswar from Delhi. I was sitting in the airport lounge, waiting for the announcement call for boarding. Next to me, an Austrian couple was sitting, waiting for the same flight. I struck up a conversation with them and came to know that they were planning to visit Odisha and South India. However, the lady was in great distress. They had arrived from Vienna only two days earlier. She was suffering not only from jet lag, but also from cold and flu. Despite taking antibiotics and other medicines, she did not get much relief. They did not want to cancel their trip, as flight tickets, hotel, and other arrangements had all been paid in advance.

Although in the airport lounge she was listening very attentively about the places of tourist attraction in Odisha, I could make out that she was fatigued and unwell. I spoke to the couple about Sai Baba, took out the packet of udi from my wallet, and gave a little bit to the lady to take, as well as to apply on her forehead. Then, with great confidence, I told her, "By evening, you will definitely feel all right."

In two hours, we reached Bhubaneswar. When I was collecting my luggage at the conveyor belt, the couple came up and thanked me profusely as the lady was feeling much better. The lady, feeling greatly relieved and cheerful, asked me, "Where can I get the powder that you had given me?" I told her, "It is no powder, but udi. This is the greatest of all medicines for any kind of disease for a true devotee of Baba. During your stay in Bhubaneswar, you can collect udi from Shirdi Sai Baba's temple located at Tankapani Road." Looking at her cheerful face and beholding the magical effect of udi given to her just two hours ago, strengthened my faith in the all- powerful udi — the panacea for all problems, be they physical or psychological.

*****

Fasting Disapproved by Sai Baba

Although Samarth Sadguru Shri Sainath was the Master of all siddhis, He never wanted to exhibit any leela or miracle. Baba never used to advise anybody to practise either any difficult yoga technique or follow any austere practice. Baba Himself never used to fast, nor did He ever ask any devotee to fast. As a matter of fact, Baba never accepted fasting, in principle, as an integral part of spiritual practice. Literally, fasting means non-acceptance of food. People who go for austere fasts do not even drink water during the period of fasting. However, Baba used to severely detest such extreme practices. In many parts of India, *upabasa* (a Sanskrit word used in many Indian languages) means fasting. But its Sanskrit source (*upa* + *basa*) means "to stay near". According to Baba, the term *upabasa* means to remain in close proximity of God. In order to attain paramartha or self-realization, or to come closer to God, one need not abstain himself from food. Whoever does fasting, which means abstaining from food and water, can never remain calm. In such a situation, how can he attain paramartha?

Baba used to say in Marathi, "*Karuniya sthira mana, payo gambhir hey dhyana,*" meaning, if the mind remains calm, the dhyana (meditation) becomes intense. If there is not even a morsel of food in the stomach and the body is famished due to starvation, how can the mind remain stable and calm? As a matter of fact, when the body is nourished with proper nutrition, then only can we practise devotion and other sadhanas for attaining God. Therefore, fasting, which involves abstinence from food, is not proper or desirable. In a similar manner, Baba also used to restrain His dear devotees from overeating. Baba has been heard telling Abdullah, a dedicated devotee of Baba, "*Eat a little, don't take varieties of dishes. Never remain on empty stomach.*" Baba was always in favour of moderation in diet. The body should consume just enough food to keep itself properly nourished—this was Baba's view.

Once a lady devotee of Baba, Mrs Gokhale, had come to Shirdi for Baba's darshan. She had brought an introductory letter from Mrs Kashibhai Kanitkar, a devotee of Baba, to Dada Kelkar, another devotee of Baba and a resident of Shirdi. She had come with a firm resolution to observe fast for three days at Baba's feet. The omniscient Baba had told Dada Kelkar the previous day itself that He would not allow His children to starve during the Shimga (Holi) festival. He said that if they had to starve what was He there for?

The next day, when Mrs. Gokhale, along with Dada Kelkar, came for Baba's darshan, Baba said to her immediately, "*What is the necessity of fasting? Go to Dadabhat's house, prepare puranpolis (wheat rotis stuffed with gram flour and jaggery), feed others, and yourself too.*" This was the time for Shimga festival. Moreover, Mrs Kelkar was unwell and there was nobody to cook in their house. So Baba's order was apt and timely. Mrs Gokhale had to abide by Baba's orders. She went to Dadabhai's house and prepared puranpolis as directed by Baba, and fed everyone including herself.

The above incident illustrates the fact that, just like a mother who takes care of her children with love, Baba also used to take care of His dear devotees. Once, another devotee of Baba had come for Baba's darshan on the auspicious occasion of Ekadashi (eleventh day of the lunar month). Being

Ekadashi, the devotee was on fast. It was time for the noon aarti. However, Baba asked the devotee to first take some food and break his fast. Since it was the Ekadashi day and also it was time for the noon aarti to commence, the devotee was most reluctant to abide by Baba's orders. But, Baba in a firm tone, said, *"The noon aarti will not commence till you have taken your food."* There was no other option before the devotee but to go to the wada and have food. The aarti commenced only after he arrived at Dwarkamayi after taking food.

Through these incidents, Baba wanted to point out that there was no correlation between God-realization and fasting. Moderation in diet, calmness of mind, and steadfast meditation, rather, are essential requirements for attaining self-realization.

*****

8

Path to Self-Realization

Although, most of His devotees had accepted Sai Baba as Sadguru and had surrendered wholeheartedly to Him, Baba has never imparted any mantra or religious instruction. Never has He attached any importance to either yoga, penance, or any rigorous religious practice. Instead, He has led His followers and devotees on the path to self-realization, either directly or indirectly, through personal examples, symbols, or stories and, at times, through gestures or mediums according to the need of the situation and the need of the person involved.

Once a photographer wanted to take a picture of Baba. Baba, through gestures, said, *"No, there is no need to take pictures."* Baba then addressed him with a beautiful piece of advice, *"You destroy the Teli's (grocer's) wall (sense of difference) between us, so that we can see and meet each other face to face."* The photographer could not comprehend the meaning of Baba's remarks. Through His remark, Baba has indicated that if we remove our ego and the difference between oneself and other, then the entire universe, the Creator and the created, all become one — this realization will dawn on us. In Baba's words, *"Don't treat anybody as a separate entity or enemy. Everyone is one and the same. Therefore, whoever comes or approaches you, don't ill-treat him. It is because of several past lives' relations that he has been drawn towards you. So try to help him as much as you can and accept him as your own."* Baba has further emphasized, "*You don't have to go too far in search of Me. If you don't identify yourself with your form, then you will realize that the consciousness that is within you is also within all creations of this universe. I am that consciousness. If you practise this principle, you will realize My all pervasive attribute and in the end you will lose your entity and become one with Me.*"

Nanasaheb Chandorkar, a highly placed revenue official in Ahmednagar district, was an ardent devotee of Baba. Nanasaheb had in-depth knowledge of Gita, Upanishads, and other religious texts. In the initial days, Nanasaheb had neither much faith in Sai Baba, nor in His omnipresence. Baba used to say, "*I am there not only in Shirdi, but also in all living creatures.*" Baba wanted Nanasaheb to realize this universal truth. One day, Baba asked him to get puranpolis, widely popular in Maharashtra. Nanasaheb went to Kopergaon, purchased puranpolis from a sweet shop and returned to Shirdi. At Shirdi, he humbly offered the puranpolis to Baba. Without touching them, Baba asked Nana to accept them as prasad. Nanasaheb was bewildered and requested Baba to eat at least one puranpoli. Baba firmly told him that He had already partaken and emphatically said, "*You are in my association for the last eighteen years, still you have not recognized me? Do you think that I am confined to three and a half cubits of body? The ants and flies who were feeding on the puranpolis are one with me.*"

Nana felt abashed and apologized to Baba. Baba's omnipresence attribute was manifested, without any ambiguity, through this incident.

During his stay in Shirdi, once Nanasaheb Chandorkar had gone to the Godavari river at Kopergaon to have a holy dip, just after the lunar eclipse. After taking a bath, he gave four annas in charity to a pariah (a low caste person from south India). At that time, far away in Shirdi, Baba, sitting at Dwarkamayi, showed the same four anna coin to His bhaktas and said that He had received the coin from

Nana. Later, when Nanasaheb came to Shirdi, the devotees enquired from Nana about his charity. Nana narrated how he had given four annas to a pariah soon after taking the holy bath in the river. All the devotees present were stunned to hear this. They realized that Baba is not confined to the boundaries of Shirdi village; He is all pervasive. Although He was physically present in Shirdi, through His yogic powers He had accepted four annas in charity from Nanasaheb at Kopergaon. A Sadguru is all powerful and all pervading. He co-exists in all animate and inanimate objects of the universe. If we surrender to him and meditate on him, the Sadguru will definitely help us in our path to self-realization.

Towards the last part of the 19th century, the glory of Sai Baba of Shirdi had spread not only in Ahmednagar district, but also in every nook and corner of Maharashtra and several parts of India, especially after the wonderful incident when Sai Baba took Samadhi and left His mortal coil and then came back to life after three days, in August 1886. The people of Shirdi and other devotees initially wondered whether Baba would ever come back alive. To remove their doubts and instill faith in them, Baba came back to normal life from the Samadhi state after three days. This miracle swept aside all questions and apprehensions about Baba's divinity. After this incident, the flow of visitors and devotees to Shirdi increased manifold. Among them, many came to Shirdi with material desires — to get relief from their miseries, pains, etc., or to get children with Baba's blessings, or to get rid of their poverty and sufferings. However, some also came with pure, spiritual desire. Belonging to various castes, creeds, and religions, the devotees and visitors flocked to Dwarkamayi in Shirdi to pay their obeisance to Baba and be blessed by Him.

Once a rich and affluent man, who aspired to get *Brahmagyan* (knowledge of Brahma) from Baba, came to Shirdi. On reaching Shirdi, he came to Dwarkamayi masjid for Baba's darshan. After paying his obeisance to Baba, he humbly requested Him to bless him with Brahmagyan. Baba replied, "*Oh My dear friend! Do not be anxious, I shall show you Brahma. Many people come to Me seeking wealth, health, power, honour, position, cure of disease, and other temporal matters. Rare is the person who comes to Me and asks for Brahmagyan. It is, indeed, a fortunate and auspicious moment that you have come here seeking for Brahmagyan. So forthwith, I will show to you Brahma with all its accompaniments and complexities.*"

Then Baba called a boy and told him to go to one Nandu Marwadi and get from him a loan of five rupees. The boy left and returned immediately, stating that Nandu Marwadi was not there and his house was locked. Then Baba asked him to go to Bala, the grocer, and get from him the loan. This time also the boy was unsuccessful. Baba repeated the task by asking the boy to visit two or three more houses, but the boy failed to procure the loan.

In the meantime, the rich man started getting impatient as he was in a hurry to return home. He implored to Baba, "Oh Baba, please give me Brahmagyan soon!" Baba replied, "*Oh My dear friend, I am doing exactly what you want. Did you not understand all the procedure that I went through sitting here at Dwarkamayi for enabling you to see Brahma? You have a bundle of five rupees notes in your pocket. If you were really sincere, you would not have been a silent spectator when I was frantically trying to get a paltry sum of five rupees. When you are not able to advance an insignificant amount of five rupees, how can you expect to attain Brahmagyan – the greatest of all things in the world?*"

The omniscient Baba had known that both Nandu Marwadi and Bala, the grocer, were not present at their homes. He only wanted to test the rich man who had come to Him seeking Brahmagyan. Then Baba explained to the rich man as follows:

For seeing Brahma, one has to surrender five things in life viz., (1) Five pranas (vital forces), (2) Five senses, (3) Mind, (4) Intellect, and (5) Ego. The path of Brahmagyan or self-realization is as difficult as treading on the edge of a razor.

There are two types of things—shreyas (the good) and preyas (the pleasant). The former deal with spiritual matters and the latter deal with mundane matters. If we do not get distracted by preyas, rather go for only shreyas in life, then the path to self-realization becomes easier and successful.

Like the sage Raman Maharishi, Sai Baba used to advise His devotees to concentrate only on one question. The question is "Who am I?" If a person believes that he is in bondage, that it is essential to get free from this bond, and in this resolution he remains absolutely firm and selflessly works without any attachment or temptation for material gains, then he is capable of spiritual evolution.

*****

9

Control over Thoughts

Once a gentleman visited Shirdi and was staying in a wada close to Dwarkamayi masjid. When he went to the masjid for Baba's darshan, Baba asked him, "*Today, in the afternoon, what were you discussing in the wada?*" The gentleman was taken by surprise and did not know what to answer. Because before coming to Dwarkamayi, in the company of his friends, he was busy criticizing and finding fault in others. He did not have the courage to admit to Baba about the topic they were discussing, so he kept quiet.

But nothing is hidden from the omniscient Baba. Although Baba was sitting in the masjid, it appeared that Baba had heard the entire conversation that had taken place in the wada. With a heavy heart, Baba said, "*Look at those pigs near the drain at Lendibagh. Behold, how and with what relish they are eating filth! Your conduct is similar. By criticizing and reviling others, you are only removing their impurities. Just like those pigs, who are enjoying the filth and dirt that they are eating, you are also enjoying by scandalizing others. After performing many deeds of merit, you are born as a human being and if you act like this, how can Shirdi help you in any way? Speaking sarcastically, criticizing or reviling others, do not help in spiritual evolution, rather they become obstructing factors. Your conduct has pained me a lot.*"

The scandal-monger learnt a lesson from Baba's stern reprimand and took to heart Baba's upright counsel. Realizing his mistake, he took a firm resolution never to revile others.

Baba used to get very annoyed when anyone used to speak ill of others due to jealousy, spite, or hatred. He would strongly reprimand and sternly give orders to root out these vices. Once, Kakasaheb Dixit, a devotee of Baba, spoke ill of Jesus Christ. After a few days, when he came to Shirdi for Baba's darshan, Baba did not allow him to enter the masjid. As he sat there in the courtyard of the masjid introspecting and evaluating his actions, he realized his mistake and was filled with remorse.

Such type of behaviour was undesirable and in order to curb and control these thoughts and inappropriate actions, Sai Baba used to give advice to His dear devotees in different ways and as required by the circumstances. A man's virtues and moral strengths are built upon years of restraint and practice. But the downfall takes no time. Sadguru Sainath used to keep strict vigil over the conduct and activities of His devotees, like a moral guardian, and this has definitely helped a number of His devotees from inevitable downfall.

Once Baba had told His dear devotee, Rao Bahadur S. B. Dhumal, "*I am taking care of you, every minute.*" The context in which Baba had spoken these words will touch the heart of every devotee. Dhumal was a lawyer from Nasik and he had come to Shirdi for Baba's darshan. After reaching Shirdi late in the evening, he decided to rest in the wada and take Baba's darshan the next morning. In the morning, when Dhumal came to the masjid, Baba fondly addressed him as *bhau* (in Marathi, *bhau* is addressed to a dear friend). Sai Baba said, "*Bhau, I could not sleep the whole night, yesterday.*" When Dhumal asked for the reason, Baba said, "*The whole night I was thinking about you. Otherwise, what would have happened to you, God only knows.*" This incident had occurred in the year 1907, when Dhumal was 34 years old, predeceased by his wife, and with no issues to take care. A successful lawyer by profession, he had no dearth of money. Under such circumstances, Baba had kept a vigilant eye on him and watched his thought and actions very carefully. In reality, Dhumal had many evil and unhealthy thoughts, which had kept troubling him the previous night. In order to save Dhumal from their evil influence, Baba had to remain alert and watchful the entire night. Such is the extent of love and compassion of a guru!

A person, who is not capable of disassociating himself from evil habits or is not able to maintain his calm and composure by keeping himself away from evil actions, will never be able to achieve self-realization. Baba has explained this very beautifully in Marathi, *"Karuniya sthira mana, payo gambhir hey dhyana."* Unfazed meditation is possible only with a calm mind. Kriyayogi Guru Lahiri Mahasaya has also said very succinctly, "Unstable mind and fickle soul can never achieve sadhana in yoga." In the words of Sadguru Sai Baba, *"Whoever is desirous of achieving sadgati* (salvation) *has to observe self-restraint, should be stable, and most important of all, should lead a life of a sadachari (right conduct)."*

*****

10

Sadguru Shows the Path

The Isha Upanishad is considered as the jewel among all the Upanishads. This Upanishad, consisting of only eighteen *shlokas*, has been able to incorporate the essence of Indian culture and heritage for which reason Gandhiji used to rate it very high. The meaning and significance of Isha Upanishad has been elucidated in its very first verse. The essence of this is as follows: God pervades every animate and inanimate object in this universe. This is the only permanent and universal truth. Therefore, one should never get attached with any object. One has to be free from all attachment and illusions in order to attain self-realization.

One of the devotees of Sai Baba, Dasganu Maharaj, wanted to translate the Isha Upanishad in Marathi language. The real name of Dasganu Maharaj was Ganpat Rao Dattatreya Sahasrabuddhe. While serving as a police constable, he was fortunate enough to get drawn towards Sai Baba. Under His divine influence, he gradually gave up his craving for power and position. He not only lost interest in his police job, but also gave up his other hobby, which was enacting different characters on stage shows by reciting *lavanis* (Marathi songs sung lasciviously). He spent the rest of his life in service of Baba, by conducting kirtans and bhajans and singing and spreading the glory of Baba in nearby provinces.

This was the start of his spiritual journey. Many of his devotional compositions have found place in Sai Aarti.

Dasganu Maharaj wrote two books, *Bhakta Leelamrit* and *Santha Kathamrit*, which are highly acclaimed in the state of Maharashtra. However, the intricacies and content of Isha Upanishad became a herculean task for Dasganu when he ventured to translate it in simple and comprehensible Marathi language. In order to understand the essence of the Isha Upanishad, he approached many learned scholars for their help. However, he was not satisfied. His friends advised that only a self-realized Sadguru could come to his rescue in this matter. With a lot of hope and faith, he came to Shirdi and pleaded for Sadguru Sai Baba's blessings to enable him to complete the noble endeavour. However, Sai Baba's answer took everyone by surprise. Instead of directly helping Dasganu with the interpretation of Isha Upanishad, He smilingly stated, *"There is no cause for anxiety. On your return journey, visit Kakasaheb Dixit's house at Ville Parle and his maidservant will solve your problem."* The people who were present in Baba's darbar thought that Baba was joking. How could an illiterate maid solve this mystical narration! But Dasganu was convinced. He was certain that Baba's word has to come true because it was the decree of Brahma.

Having full faith in Baba, he left Shirdi with Baba's blessings and came to Ville Parle, a suburb of Mumbai, and stayed with Kakasaheb Dixit. The next day, when he woke up, he heard a beautiful song in a sweet and melodious voice. When he looked through the window, he saw Kakasaheb's maidservant singing a song while cleaning utensils. The girl was wearing a torn saree, but looked very cheerful. The song was about a crimson coloured silk saree, with beautiful golden borders, and fine embroidery. Dasganu was surprised to see her cheerful demeanour despite her poverty. At the same time, he felt pity for her and thought about how delighted she would be if she were to be gifted a saree exactly like the one she was singing about. He requested Kakasaheb to get a crimson coloured silk saree with a golden embroidered border for him. Kakasaheb procured it through

M. V. Pradhan. When Dasganu gave it to the maid, her joy knew no bounds.

The next day, the girl wore the new saree and danced with great joy, showing it to her friends. The following day she kept the new saree at home and came in her old and torn saree. However, she looked as happy as she was on the previous day and performed all household chores cheerfully. Dasganu saw that although the girl was poor, she showed no signs of being sad or miserable.

Dasganu's pity, then, transformed into admiration. It immediately dawned on him that all our feelings of pain and pleasure depend upon the attitude of our mind. He received a practical demonstration of the lesson from the Upanishad from the behaviour of the young maid. The young girl, though very poor, was equally happy and cheerful before receiving the new saree as well as after receiving it. Dasganu understood that happiness is a state of mind. We should be contented with what we have got because everything is ordained by God. In this particular case, the impoverished condition of the poor girl, her torn saree and the new saree, the donor, and the donee — all constitute actions of the Lord. "God pervades everything" is the ultimate truth which should be realized by everyone. Once it is realized, then we will have love, affection for others, infatuation and hatred for none, and we will not covet others' wealth.

*****

11

All Faiths Lead to God

Sai Baba lived in Shirdi for a period of 60 years, from 1858 to 1918, that is, till he attained *mahasamadhi*. In those days, Shirdi was a small and nondescript village in Kopergaon Taluk of Ahmednagar district in the state of Maharashtra. Baba had made an old, abandoned, and dilapidated masjid His home and had fondly named it Dwarkamayi. According to Baba, "*Dwarkamayi is everybody's mother. Just like an infant who is sheltered and protected from all obstacles and troubles in the lap of its mother, similarly, whoever takes shelter in the lap of Dwarkamayi, is free from all troubles. Whoever climbs the steps of the masjid, however poor he may be, all his troubles come to an end and he is filled with infinite joy.*"

The doors of Dwarkamayi were open to all — the oppressed, the untouchables, the rich, or the poor. People, irrespective of caste, creed, or religion, were drawn towards Sai Baba and visited Shirdi to assemble in the courtyard of Dwarkamayi just to have a glimpse of Sai Baba and be blessed by him. The last part of the nineteenth century and the first two decades of the twentieth century were witness to how India was torn by religious strife and communal tension. It was during this period that Baba used to draw devotees from all religions — Hindus, Muslims, Parsis, Christians — and they would assemble in the darbar of Baba, blissfully enjoying His divine company.

Baba used to sit, most of the time, in Dwarkamayi in front of the dhuni, which was perpetually burning, in the manner of a true Agnihotri Brahmin. Every day, He would go begging for alms from a few houses in Shirdi village. Whatever food He collected, He would first offer it to the sacred dhuni and then share it with devotees as well as the stray animals like cats and dogs, and even birds. It is a well-known fact that fire is the revered God for the Parsis. Just like the Hindus who conduct marriages and thread ceremony before the fire god, the Parsis also perform all sacred functions before the fire deity with great reverence.

Baba's attire was such that many people used to think that He was a Muslim fakir. Baba used to wear a kafni, tie a piece of white cloth over His head, and carry a satka (short stick). These were His only material possessions, besides a jholi and a tumrel. The jholi was used to collect dry food and the tumrel was meant for liquid food, whenever Baba would go on His begging rounds. Baba also used to wear a *koupin* (codpiece) like any other yogi and to those devotees who wanted to embrace sanyaas, there are instances of Sai Baba gifting them His koupin. In the courtyard of the masjid and in the wada, people belonging to different religions used to read holy books of their own religion.

Baba often used to repeat "*Allah Malik hai*" meaning that God is supreme and at the time of blessing His devotees He would say, "*Allah tera bhala karega,*" meaning that God will do good things for you. Baba used to allow His Hindu devotees to apply sandalwood paste on His forehead, to perform aarti and puja in the masjid, and to sing bhajans and kirtans inside Dwarkamayi. The period Baba lived in Shirdi was marked by a high degree of communal rift between the Hindus and Muslims and each one was critical of the mode of worship of the other. Once, a Muslim devotee called Rangari asked Baba, "Why are the Hindu devotees of yours applying sandalwood paste on your forehead? This is against our religion." Hearing this Baba answered, "*Jaisa desh waisa bhesh*" implying that we should adapt ourselves to the society we live in and follow its customs and practices. He said, *"My Hindu devotees treat Me as their God and offer prayers to Me. Why should I displease them by refusing? I am Myself a servant of God."*

Shri Sainath always used to advise that Ram and Rahim are one and there exist no difference between the two. Therefore, their devotees should not fight among themselves. Baba not only used to show respect and tolerance for both the religions, Hinduism and Islam, alike but also used to exhibit high degree of regard for other religions, too. Once, at Rahata Police Station (Rahata is the adjoining village of Shirdi), a Christian police officer was posted as officer-in-charge. Some of Baba's devotees approached Baba and said, "We have now got a Christian police officer." Baba instantly replied, *"So what, he is my brother."*

Baba expected that all His devotees should exhibit tolerance and respect for other religions. Once, Kakasaheb Dixit, a dear devotee of Sai Baba, had spoken ill of Jesus Christ. After a few days, when Kaka visited Shirdi, Baba did not permit him to do *padaseva,* nor did He talk to him. He just kept mum. He did not even allow him to enter the masjid. Kakasaheb was taken aback by Baba's indifferent behaviour. As he introspected over his past actions, he realized his mistake and was filled with remorse. Later, when Kaka begged for forgiveness for his improper remarks, Baba forgave him and embraced him.

The most amazing fact was the simultaneous celebration of the Ramnavami festival by the Hindu devotees and the Urs festival by the Muslim devotees, at Shirdi, during Baba's time. Both the festivals were observed on the same day with great fervour and spirit. This would not have been possible at all without the encouragement and divine blessings of Sai Baba.

Shri Sainath used to participate in the bhajans and kirtans conducted by the Hindu devotees. During Muhharam, He used to allow His Muslim devotees to put up *Taziya* in front of the masjid, as well as to conduct the symbolic chandan yatra. From all this, we can infer that Baba used to give His consent to His devotees for celebrating festivals on the basis of their devotion and faith. While He used to encourage His faithful devotee, Abdullah, to read the holy Quran in the masjid, He also used to participate very enthusiastically in discussions about the Upanishads and Gita with Nanasaheb Chandorkar.

Sai Baba was very much against changing one's own religion. Once Bade Baba, an old Muslim fakir residing in Shirdi, brought a Hindu, who had converted into a Muslim, before Baba. Baba, on meeting this person, slapped him on his face and asked, "*How could you change your father?*" The act of conversion was strongly reprimanded by Baba. He always used to advise that we should never give up our religion, we should never stop praying to one's *Ishtadeva* (family deity), and we should not change our guru.

*****

12

How Baba Used to Protect
His Devotees

In 1911 Shirdi was affected by plague, which became an epidemic. At that time, Sai Baba also suffered from the disease and His body was covered with several buboes. His devotees became very concerned and asked Baba the remedy for the disease. Baba told them not to be frightened at the sight of the buboes and assured them that the buboes would subside quickly. He also said that the buboes would disappear when cotton wool soaked in warm ghee was applied on them. He told His devotees that no one in Shirdi would have any fatal consequences because of the plague.

Baba's words came true as nobody in Shirdi succumbed to the plague. It was the firm belief of the villagers that whenever any calamity befell Shirdi, Baba bore the brunt of the calamity Himself and saved the village folk. He protected them from every kind of disaster. The most surprising fact was that in spite of Baba suffering from bubonic plague, He remained calm and composed and carried out His daily routine, like going on His peregrination rounds, begging from house to house, visiting the Lendibagh twice a day—once in the morning and once in the evening—as well as spending hours in the company of His dear devotees in the darbar at Dwarkamayi masjid. All these activities were a part of Baba's daily routine.

The author of Shri Sai Satcharita, Shri Annasaheb Dabholkar alias Hemadpant, visited Shirdi for the first time in the year 1910. He was so much inspired by the divine personality of Sai Baba and the rare sight he chanced to behold on his arrival at Shirdi, that he was motivated to write a book on His wonderful life and teachings. At that time, Shirdi and the neighbouring villages were ravaged by cholera and the disease was spreading fast. One fine morning, Baba, after finishing His daily chores, sat down in the courtyard of Dwarkamayi and started grinding wheat. The village folks were amazed to find Baba grinding wheat. They wondered as to of what use was the flour to Baba, since He lived on alms. Suddenly, four ladies from among the crowd approached Baba. They gently pushed Baba aside and took over the work of grinding. At first, Baba was enraged at their intrusion. But observing their devotion and dedication, He smiled at them and allowed them to continue the grinding. Once the grinding was over, the ladies made four portions of the flour, with an intention to take it home, since they presumed that Baba would have no use for it. Baba strongly objected and directed them to spread the flour along the borders of Shirdi village. Annasaheb, who was watching the entire incident with curiosity, asked the village folks the significance of Baba's orders. They replied that it was Baba's method of controlling the cholera epidemic in Shirdi and its adjoining areas. Soon after this incident, it was found that the intensity of the disease declined. The villagers of Shirdi believed that grinding wheat was only symbolic and, in reality, Baba was grinding cholera and driving it away from Shirdi.

The ever compassionate Baba, who was committed to the welfare of His devotees, had dedicated His entire life for their protection and welfare. Annasaheb Dabholkar was simply awestruck by Baba's incredible method of cure and was inspired to write the life of such a divine and magnificent personality.

Dadasaheb Khaparde, a reputed advocate of Amravati, visited Shirdi along with his family in the year 1911 and stayed for almost four months. During that time Shirdi was affected by plague. One day Khaparde's young son suffered from high fever and developed some buboes on his body. Smt. Khaparde got very scared. As, at that time, Shirdi was woefully lacking in medical facilities, she ran to Baba, her rescuer and prayed to Him to save her son. Sai Baba, in a compassionate tone, said, "*Mother, don't be afraid. The sky is overcast. Very soon it will start raining and the dark clouds will disappear. Shirdi is your saviour. I take upon myself the pains and sufferings of my children.*" So saying, Baba lifted up His kafni up to the waist and showed to all present, four fully developed buboes. Tears of gratitude flowed down Smt. Khaparde's face and she bowed down in *sastang pranam* to Baba. Her son started getting well from that very moment.

Even far away from Shirdi, the pitiful cries and fervent prayers of Baba's devotees to rescue them from difficulties, anguish, pain, and so on, never went unheard. The ever-merciful Baba would always come to the rescue of His dear devotees. Once, Baba was sitting in front of the dhuni along with other devotees when, suddenly, He thrust his hand into the dhuni. Even though His hand got scorched in the flames, Baba was not bothered and remained calm as if nothing untoward had happened. This was noticed by Madhav, an errand boy, and Shama, the school teacher. They, at once, dragged Baba away forcibly. But the damage had already been done. They were very puzzled and asked Baba to explain His strange behaviour. Then Baba came to His senses and replied, "*I do not mind My hand getting burnt. However, I am glad that the child could be saved.*" After some days, this mystery was unfolded to all. Far away from Shirdi, the wife of a blacksmith was working at the furnace with her child in her lap, when her husband called her. Forgetting that the child was in her lap, she got up hastily and the child slipped into the furnace. Piteously and fervently she prayed to Baba to save her child. Responding to her prayers, Baba thrust His hand into the dhuni in order to take the child out of the fire. In the process, though Baba's hand got burnt, the child was saved, to the great relief of the mother.

Although Baba used to lead a very simple and unostentatious life of a fakir and remained busy in His daily routine work like going on His begging rounds, grooming the Lendibagh, taking care of the sick and the disabled, He was ever eager to come to the rescue of His dear devotees who prayed to Him sincerely and with devotion.

Sai Baba's life is an exemplary tale of never-ending compassion and incredible sacrifice, rendered and exhibited through His wonderful leelas. During Baba's sojourn in Shirdi, many visitors and devotees came to Him to fulfil their materialistic desires. Some devotees came with spiritual yearnings. They would narrate their tales of woe, their pains and anguish, their sorrows and sufferings, and would seek Baba's blessings. In turn, Baba would dedicate His time and energy for ensuring their welfare. He would take upon Himself their pains and sufferings, without a murmur.

In the initial days, at times, Baba cooked food Himself and fed all who were present in the masjid. Gradually, as Baba's name and fame began to spread to different parts of the country, people visited Shirdi in large numbers. They also brought with them fruits and food items for naivedya. However, Baba never stopped begging till He breathed His last. Every day, He used to visit three or four houses of Shirdi village and beg for alms. Begging was not only an integral part of His sanyaasi life, but by begging from those few, known houses of Shirdi, Baba would enquire about their welfare, as well as bless them. This practice had been developed into a daily routine and Baba regarded this routine as His duty towards His devotees.

When Baba sat in the masjid in the company of His devotees, He would get engrossed in listening to their mundane problems, talking to them, joking with them, and giving solace to their afflicted souls. Baba indicated to His devotees time and again that He was their eternal companion both in times of happiness and sorrow, as well as in the present life and the life after.

Baba's words have always proved to be true, when Baba was in His mortal coil as well as after His mahasamadhi. Baba had assured His dear devotee Kakasaheb Dixit, "*All your worries are Mine and I accept your entire responsibility.*" When Baba was uttering these words, at that very moment, Kakasaheb's daughter, who was playing at their home in Bandra (Mumbai), climbed up an almirah to get some dolls which were placed there. She accidentally tripped and fell and the almirah fell on top of her. But to the amazement of all family members, she escaped from this grave accident without any serious injury. There were just a few bruises and scratches on her hands due to the impact of her fall.

In another incident, Baba was sitting in His darbar, busy listening to the woes of His devotees, when all of a sudden, He got up and made a noise similar to the blowing of a conch shell sounding a death knell. Then He spoke, "*Nana is in danger. But should I allow My Nana to die? I have to save him.*" At that time, Nanasaheb Chandorkar, a highly placed revenue official in Ahmednagar district, was travelling in a tonga, along with an acquaintance. The horses were running at a very high speed. Suddenly, Nana lost his balance and fell from the tonga. But because of Baba's ever protecting support, Nana and his co-traveller could be saved from this accident without any injury. The omniscient Baba's loving care and protection for His devotees is clearly evident from this incident.

Baba had also made a promise to Kakasaheb Dixit saying, "*I shall take my Kaka in a biman (aeroplane,)*," which implies that Baba would give Kaka sadgati. This has been proved true. Eight years after Baba's mahasamadhi, in 1926, Kakasaheb

Dixit was travelling in a train with Annasaheb Dhabolkar, the author of Shri Sai Satcharita. He was deeply engrossed in a discussion relating to Baba and His leelas with Annasaheb, when suddenly, he breathed his last and fell on Anna's shoulders. Indeed, Baba had showered sadgati on His Kaka as promised. Sadgati can only be attained with the blessings of a Samarth Sadguru like Sainath.

Captain Jehangir Daruwala was a Parsi devotee of Baba and a sea-trader, by profession. Once, he had gone on a voyage, along with his fleet of ships. He was at deep sea when he encountered a terrible storm. There was the imminent danger of the ships sinking, so he prayed to Baba to come to his rescue. Holding tightly Baba's photo to his chest, tears rolled down his eyes relentlessly and he prayed fervently to Baba to save his ships from sinking. At that moment, Baba was sitting in front of the dhuni at Dwarkamayi. The devotees present there observed that all of a sudden, water started to flow incessantly from Baba's kafni and His turban. They were amazed to see this sight. Three days later, a telegram reached Shirdi. The content of the telegram was that Captain Jehangir and his fleet of ships had reached the shore, safe and sound. After a few days, Captain Jehangir paid a visit to Shirdi to offer his obeisance and profound gratitude to Baba, his saviour.

It has been mentioned in Vishnu Sahasranaam, "*Sulabha Subrata Siddha Shatrujit Shatrutapana,*" meaning the Almighty Lord is omnipotent, all powerful, can win over the enemies, as well as control all the evil forces in the universe. Shirdi Sai Baba, the greatest avatar (incarnation) of Kaliyuga, has always extended His hands to bless and take care of His devotees. In return, He expected them to offer their sincere devotion and faith. Shri Sainath has often said to His devotees, "*Whoever comes to Me and wholeheartedly surrenders to Me, or seeks My protection, I shall remain ever alert and active in helping him as well as showing him the right path. If required, I may take birth life after life in order to redeem them.*" It is evident from the experiences of many devotees that Baba, even after taking mahasamadhi, is not only controlling the thoughts and actions of His devotees but also protecting them all the time.

When Baba was in His mortal coil and residing in Shirdi, it was possible for Him to send udi for pregnant Mainatai, the daughter of Nanasaheb Chandorkar, a highly placed revenue official in Ahmednagar district, as well as save the young daughter of Kakasaheb Dixit, a solicitor of Mumbai, staying at his Bandra residence. Similarly, there are innumerable incidents which amply substantiate the fact that even after leaving His mortal coil, Baba has been reaching out to His devotees to answer their earnest prayers and bail them out from their difficulties and problems. Rao Bahadur S. B. Dhumal, a devotee of Baba has said, "There is no incident, small or big, that has taken place in my life in which I have not involved Baba. I think, the course of my life is controlled and guided by Baba. Even today, Baba is still active and vigorous although He has taken mahasamadhi." This statement was made to Shri B. V. Narasimha Swami in the year 1936 by Shri Dhumal, although Sai Baba had already taken mahasamadhi in the year 1918. Shri Dhumal had earned the love and affection of Baba by dint of his unflinching devotion and dedication. Once Baba had told him, "*I am taking care of you at every step of yours.*"

An incident can be narrated, which shows how Baba cares for His devotees and comes to their rescue in times of need. A Sai devotee, Dr Purna Chandra Mishra had this wonderful experience of how Baba rescued his daughter from the jaws of death. In the year 1985, his daughter met with a road accident at Buxi Bazaar in Cuttack city, where she was hit by a speeding vehicle. The impact resulted in her being thrown away to a distance of five to six feet. However, her life was saved and there was no injury. At that time, Dr Mishra, who was posted to the remote district of Koraput, was having his afternoon siesta, since it was a Sunday. He dreamt that Baba was holding his daughter in His arms. What a wonderful miracle!

The following incident has already been narrated in the periodical *Sai Leela,* which is the esteemed publication of Shirdi Sai Sansthan. This wonderful incident is largely responsible for the establishment of a beautiful Sai Temple in Mauritius. The head-driver of Mauritius Municipal Corporation had a son who was deaf and dumb since birth. On the recommendation of well-wishers, he brought his son to India and visited several holy places. At the end of his pilgrimage, he happened to visit Shirdi, the abode of Samarth Sadguru Shri Sai Baba. As the child kneeled down and bowed at the Samadhi of Baba, a miracle happened. Everybody present could hear a feeble sound calling "Maa". His parents were astonished at this development and a glimmer of hope appeared in their minds. Later, the child started speaking, with the divine grace of Sai Baba. With profound gratitude to Baba, he left Shirdi, a happy man. With generous contributions from several Sai devotees, he took upon the task of constructing a temple for Sainath. This temple is one of the key destinations for any visitor to Mauritius.

To the ordinary mind, the incidents narrated above may sound miraculous, but those Sai devotees who have read about Param Sadguru Shri Sai know that Baba had all the siddhis which He used for mitigating the afflictions and miseries of devotees who had surrendered to Him. In fact, He regarded service to the poor and afflicted persons and protection of devotees as *Bhagwad Seva* (divine service). Whenever any devotee used to express his gratitude after the fulfilment of his desire or alleviation of his misery, Baba used to say, without any trace of ego, *"Rather, I am fortunate enough to serve you and for that, I am ever grateful to God."*

*****

13

Naam Smaran

Param Sadguru Shri Sai Baba of Shirdi used to inspire and initiate different devotees in different ways to follow the path of self-realization according to their inclinations, virtues, and tendencies. Madhavrao Deshpande was a dear devotee who Baba used to fondly address as Shama. He worked as a teacher in a primary school at Shirdi. After school hours he used to spend the rest of the time mostly in the service of Baba. For Shama, Sai Baba was his friend, philosopher, and guide. To remain forever in the service of Baba and to carry out Baba's orders, letter by letter, was the primary objective of his life.

Once a Ramdaasi (disciple of Saint Ramdas) visited Shirdi and stayed there for some time. Every day, after finishing his daily chores, he would read the Vishnu Sahasranaam and Adhyatma Ramayan with full devotion and sincerity. Sai Baba wanted His dear Shama to read the Vishnu Sahasranaam text which has one thousand names of Lord Vishnu. So, one day He summoned the Ramdaasi and said, "*I am having severe stomach ache. Go to the market immediately and get sonamukhi (medicine for stomach disorder) for Me. I will get relief only after taking sonamukhi.*" The Ramdaasi had to stop reading and go to the market to get sonamukhi in obedience to Baba's orders. Then Baba got up from His seat, picked up the Vishnu Sahasranaam text which the Ramdaasi had been reading, handed it over to Shama, and said, "*This book is very valuable and efficacious. So I am giving it to you to read. Once I went through miserable pain and my life was in danger. At that critical moment, I hugged the book close to my heart and what a relief it gave to me! I felt as if God Himself had come to my rescue. This is why I am giving this book to you. You should read at least one name daily and it will do you good."* However, since the Ramdaasi was an ill-tempered and obstinate person, Shama felt that if he took the book from Baba, the Ramdaasi would definitely quarrel with him. Secondly, Shama was not very proficient in Sanskrit, the language in which the book was written. He thought that his deficiency may be an obstacle in reading Vishnu Sahsranaam and, moreover, he may not be able to understand the meaning and significance underlying the text. Keeping these factors in mind, Shama did not take the book. However, the ever compassionate Sai had greater visions for Shama. He wanted to gift him Vishnu Sahsranaam because it would not only purify his mind but also save him from worldly miseries.

Everybody knows the greatness of God's name and the benefit received by simply uttering it. The significance of uttering God's name has also been mentioned in Vishnu Sahasranaam text as follows:

Anybody who recites or remembers God's name daily will never face any problems or difficulties in this world or in the other world.

Naam smaran (remembering God's name) saves us from all evil and bad habits and frees us from the bondage of the cycle of birth and death. Although Shama was not very keen to accept Vishnu Sahasranaam from Baba, He was very eager that Shama should read the book daily, which was essential for Shama's spiritual development. Therefore, He thrust the book in Shama's hands and ordered him to read it every day.

After some time, the Ramdaasi returned from the market with the sonamukhi. Soon he came to know that his book was in Shama's possession. He was enraged and burst upon Shama with anger. He accused Shama of plotting against him. He thought it was Shama who had set up Baba to send him to the market to get sonamukhi, under the pretext of a stomach ache. He felt Shama had planned all this with the intention of taking away his book. Shama tried to pacify the furious Ramdaasi by explaining to him that his allegations were false and baseless. However, the Ramdaasi did not calm down and threatened to break his head if his book was not returned to him. Sai Baba was watching the entire proceedings with amusement. Then Baba spoke kindly to the Ramdaasi, *"Oh Ramdaasi, what is the matter with you? Why are you so furious, even though you are a devotee of Shri Ram? How come you can be so quarrelsome? Can you not speak in a soft and tender tone? You are reading this sacred book every day, still your mind is so agitated and you have no control over your tongue? What sort of a Ramdaasi are you! You ought to be indifferent to all things. A true Ramdaasi should have no attachments. Your attachment to the book really puzzles me. You can buy several books with money but you cannot buy men; think well and consider the case unbiasedly. Shama had no greed for the book. You know it in your heart. I wanted Shama to benefit from reading Vishnu Sahasranaam and so I gave it to him."*

Baba's sweet and nectar-like words had a wonderful, soothing effect on the agitated Ramdaasi and he immediately calmed down.

Baba's unique method of teaching and initiating His devotees is evident from the above incident. Baba did not approve of the improper behaviour of the Ramdaasi and wanted him to change his behaviour. Therefore, He taught him through this incident that a Ramdaasi should not have any attachment for worldly possessions and should never exhibit improper behaviour. Rather, his mind should be calm and he should have control over his emotions.

Another important lesson which can be derived from this incident is that by reading the sacred book, Vishnu Sahasranaam, one's mind and body gets purified and one develops all the virtues like patience, forgiveness, self-control, and so on, which are all enabling factors for reaching self-realization.

*****

14

Gaining Knowledge from Guru

Nanasaheb Chandorkar was a very dear devotee of Sai Baba. He was a man of great stature and learning and had steadfast devotion towards Baba. He had profound knowledge of the Shastras and the Vedas, as well as the Gita and the Upanishads. He was a highly placed official in the Government and was a man of dignity and reputation. However, he was very modest and had accepted Sai Baba as his Guru and God. Whenever he had an opportunity to visit Shirdi, he would gladly go to pay his obeisance to his Lord as well as to participate in Baba's darbar. Also, he would quench his thirst for knowledge by clearing his doubts and apprehensions from the omniscient Sai Baba.

Once, while massaging Baba's feet, Nanasaheb was reciting a Sanskrit shloka in a very soft and feeble voice. The omniscient Sai Baba knew that Nana was reciting a shloka from Shrimad Bhagwad Gita in which it has been elucidated how to derive lessons (knowledge) from the guru. However, feigning ignorance, He asked Nana, *"What are you mumbling to yourself?"*

Nana: "I am reciting a shloka."
Baba: *"What shloka?"*
Nana: "From Bhagwad Gita."
Baba: *"Recite it loudly."*

Nana recited the shloka which was as follows:

Tadviddhi Pranipaatena Pariprashnena Sevaya, Upade Kshyanti Te Gyanam Gyaninastattwadarshinah.

Nana believed that Baba had never studied Sanskrit. So, he was hesitant to recite the shloka, but on Baba's insistence he did so. Although Sadguru Sai Baba was omniscient, He never exhibited His knowledge, unless required. He remained as a humble fakir and regarded Himself as a servant of God. He was a master of the Vedas, Upanishads, and had control over the entire universe, but He never displayed His authority. The devotees who had surrendered themselves to Baba were fortunate enough to be led to the path of truth and righteousness by none other than Baba Himself.

Baba asked Nana to explain the shloka, word by word. Wonderful was the conversation between them, which can be narrated as follows:

Baba: *"Nana, have you understood the shloka?"*

Nana: "Yes."

Baba: *"If so, explain its meaning!"*

Nana: "It means: Making sastang namaskar, that is, prostrating to your guru, serving him, obeying him, and acquiring knowledge from him. Because it is the guru, who has already achieved Brahmagyan and only he can instruct and impart knowledge to his disciple."

But Baba was not satisfied with Nana's explanation.

Baba: *"Nana, I do not want this sort of collected purport of the whole stanza. Give me each word, its grammatical meaning, and significance."*

Nana, who was a highly knowledgeable person and proficient in Sanskrit, was amazed at Baba's query.

Baba again asked Nana: *"Is it enough to merely making prostration?"*

Nana was confused and replied: "I do not know any other meaning for the word *Pranipaat* than making prostration."

Baba: *"What is Pariprashna?"*

Nana: "Asking questions."

Baba: *"What does prashna mean?"*

Nana   : "The same."

Baba: *"If pariprashna and prashna mean the same, why did Vyasa add the prefix pari? Was Vyasa off his head?"*

Nana: "I do not know of any other meaning for the word *pariprashna*."

Baba again asked: *"What sort of seva is referred here?"*

Nana: "Just what we are doing to you, that is, *padaseva*."

Baba: *"Is it enough to render such service?"*

Nana: "I do not know what more is signified by the word *seva*."

Nana was taken aback when Baba pressed him with questions from the shloka he had recited. Nana's pride that he was very knowledgeable and had proficiency in Sanskrit language was broken. He felt embarrassed at his deficiency. Baba had deliberately asked the questions in order to remove Nana's vanity and pride. In fact, it is the duty of a Sadguru to get rid of his disciple's pride and vanity, which become obstacles in the path of self-realization.

Baba, then, in a soft and tender tone explained to Nanasaheb, *"Firstly, it is not enough to merely prostrate before gyanis. We must surrender ourselves completely to the Sadguru. For that purpose, it is advised to take recourse to Navadha Bhakti. Navadha Bhakti constitutes nine types of bhakti, viz., (i) Shravan (hearing); (ii) Kirtan (praying); (iii) Smaran (remembering); (iv) Padasevan (resorting to the feet); (v) Archan (worship);*

(vi) Namaskar (bowing); (vii) Dasya (service); (viii) Sakhyam (friendship); (ix) Atmanivedan (surrender of the self). If any of these is faithfully followed, Lord Hari will be pleased and the devotee will be blessed. Surrender of the self implies surrender of all the faculties, be it physical or mental, to the Lord. Such a surrender is synonymous with complete surrender.

"Secondly, mere questioning is not enough. The question must not be asked with the intention to belittle the guru or out of mere curiosity. Questions should be asked with faith and devotion for clearing doubts in the path of spiritual evolution. The question should be earnest, with a view to achieve spiritual upliftment.

"Thirdly, seva is not rendering service with the feeling that one will offer service only when there is a desire, otherwise not. If this feeling remains in the mind, then it does not become a service at all. When one realizes that the body, mind, wealth, etc., all belong to the guru and one should surrender every possession in the service of the guru, then that service is, in true sense, service to God."

It is the guru who can impart *gyan* and it is he who can show the path of self-realization. So if a disciple, surrenders completely to his guru and dedicatedly serves him with faith and devotion, then he is sure to be blessed by his guru, who is God's representative on earth. A disciple remains in the delusion that he is a separate entity with a body, soul, and ego and the universe or God is separate from him. This delusion is the result of the cycle of life and death and the *sanskar* (the impressions) accumulated over several past lives. It is the guru who removes this veil of delusion and ignorance and illuminates the disciple's life with knowledge, as well as helps him to tread the path of spirituality.

*****

15

Control Over Desires Is the Key to Happiness

In the second chapter of the Bhagwad Gita, it has been clearly mentioned that just as the sea remains calm and still, despite the fact that several rivers merge into it, in a similar manner, a person with equanimity does not get ruffled by any desire, sensual or material. This means that he is above all materialistic distractions and, therefore, is always at peace, both inwardly as well as outwardly and remains forever in a blissful state. However, a person who always remains engrossed in materialistic pursuits is devoid of such bliss.

Yogeshwar Shri Sai Baba had made a small, unknown village called Shirdi His abode. He lived in an old and dilapidated masjid and spent most of His time there in the company of His devotees, who were very dear to Him and He shared their problems and anguish. Shirdi, at that time, was a nondescript village in Ahmednagar district of Maharashtra. Every day, Baba used to go on His begging rounds. He would beg from three or four houses in the village. Toward the end of nineteenth century, Baba's fame began to spread to different parts of the country and in the first two decades of twentieth century, people began visiting Shirdi in large numbers to get a glimpse of this divine personality and be blessed by Him. The devotees who came for Baba's darshan brought with them fruits, cooked food, and delicacies and sweet-meats, which were offered to Baba as naivedya with utmost devotion.

Once, one of Baba's dear devotees, out of curiosity, enquired from Baba, "Baba, so many devotees come to You for Your darshan. They get plenty of food and offer it to You as prasad. Why do You still have to go to beg every day?" Baba replied, *"Begging is an integral part of the life of a sanyasi* (one who has renounced the world). *So long as I remain in this physical body, I shall continue my work of begging."* In reality, this statement is a reflection of the egoless-ness of Sai Baba and the spartan life that He used to lead. Sai Baba of Shirdi is the greatest yogi of all times who has led millions of devotees to the path of self-realization, because He Himself was a self-realized soul. He was the greatest of fakirs and was totally unaffected by worldly possessions. He was devoid of any sensual or materialistic desire and thereby was an epitome of *stithapragyan* (equanimity).

In the above context, an incident related to Damodar Sawalram Rasne can be narrated, which illustrates how Baba used to dissuade His dear devotees from being lured by temptations of materialistic possessions. Damodar, a devotee of Baba, was a resident of Ahmednagar district. Baba was very fond of Damodar and used to address him as Damu Anna (Anna is a Marathi endearment for elder brother). Although he had two wives, he did not have any children. He had consulted several astrologers and he had also studied astrology. He found that because of inauspicious planetary positions in his horoscope, there was no chance of getting any children. Deeply disappointed, he fell at Baba's feet and begged for His blessings. The benevolent Baba blessed him and gave four mangoes, with the instruction that the mangoes should be eaten by his second wife only. In course of time, Baba's blessings came true and the astrological predictions were proved false. Thereafter, Damu Anna had immense faith in Baba.

In another incident, Damu Anna was counselled by his friend from Mumbai to invest money in cotton business. The friend convinced Damu Anna that he could reap huge profits out of this investment. Before taking the plunge, Damu Anna was keen to know Baba's view on this matter. Therefore, explaining details of the cotton business, he wrote a letter to Shama, another devotee of Baba, and requested him to seek Baba's advice on his behalf. Shama, on receiving the letter, approached Baba in the masjid and placed the letter at His feet. Baba enquired about the letter. Shama explained that Damu Anna of Ahmednagar wanted His advice on some business matter. Before Shama could open the letter and read out its contents, Baba murmured to Himself, "*It seems, he is not satisfied with whatever God has bestowed upon him. He wants to reach the sky; anyway, read out the letter.*" Shama read out the letter. Baba heard very attentively and then spoke in a very soft voice, "*Damu Seth has gone mad. Write to him and inform that since there is no dearth of things in his house, he should be satisfied with half the roti that he has at present and should not bother about lakhs.*" Shama, accordingly, wrote a letter to Damu Anna. When Damu Anna received the letter and came to know of Baba's views in the matter, he was disappointed. All his plans of making lakhs of rupees as profits in the cotton venture were shattered. However, since he was hopeful of making profits, he left for Shirdi to convince Baba of his business plans. At Shirdi, he prostrated at Baba's feet and started massaging His feet. He was wondering how to put his business proposal before Baba for reconsideration. He had made up his mind to donate a part of the profits, which he hoped to receive from the business venture, to Baba. Before he could express his thoughts, the omniscient Baba told him in a clear and firm tone, "*Anna, I don't want to be entangled with any such worldly or materialistic gains. I have nothing to do with your profit or loss. However, I have advised you whatever is good for you.*" It is evident that Baba had read the thoughts going on in Damu Anna's mind. Nothing could be concealed from the omniscient Baba—neither the past, nor the present, nor the future. Baba's outright disapproval made Damu Anna to give up the project. Soon the news came that the speculation in cotton, which was done by his friend, in association with another businessman since Damu Anna did not participate, failed and in the process they had to incur huge losses. Damu Anna realized that Baba had saved him from certain bankruptcy. Damu Anna's faith in Baba grew stronger and he was very grateful to Baba to have rescued him from such a great disaster. He remained a true devotee of Baba all his life.

A mother is always concerned about the welfare of her child. She coaxes her child to take bitter pills. She knows well that the pills will improve the health in the long run, although the child longs for sweets which will only spoil the health. In the same manner, kind-hearted Baba, knowing well the present and future prospects of His devotees, used to impart the right advice and guide them. In doing so, He did not have even the slightest vested interest. Baba had conquered all the vices like lust, greed, attachment, etc. He was always calm and composed and a repository of wisdom and virtues. Above all, He had no attraction towards any temporal or mundane possession.

Once, the Police Inspector of Kopergaon, Shri Gopal Rao Gund, decided to get repair work done of the dilapidated Dwarkamayi. Shri Gund had been blessed by Baba with a son, after several years of marriage. Out of gratitude, Shri Gund wanted to serve Baba in a humble way. So he collected the necessary construction material and was about to start the repair work, when Baba objected and said, "*I am happy in whatever condition Dwarkamayi is at present I do not want any lavish abode, nor any unnecessary articles for my living.*"

In reality, Sai Baba epitomized simplicity, humility, and egolessness, for which he was adored by one and all. It has been mentioned in Gita that one who is humble, non-egoist, has surrendered all types of desires and lust, and is totally indifferent to this mundane existence, is sure to attain supreme bliss.

*****

16

The Significance of Naam Japa

To attain God-realization, several ways and means have been mentioned in the Shastras. In the Gita, Yogeshwar Shri Krishna has spoken to Arjun on the different forms of yoga like Sankhya Yoga, Karma Yoga, Gyan-Vigyan Yoga, Dhyan Yoga, and so on, in vivid detail. The principles of Vedas, how to achieve all the chief objects of life like *Dharma* (righteousness), *Artha* (wealth), *Kama* (desire), and *Moksha* (deliverance) through worship and *yagna* have also been illustrated in the Gita. Even in this busy materialistic world, how to achieve self-realization by adopting a simple and easy method has been laid down by great saints and seers like Sai Baba of Shirdi, Ramakrishna Paramhansa, and Chaitanya Mahaprabhu for their disciples and devotees. Shri Ramakrishna Paramhansa, who spent twelve years in deep meditation and yoga practice, has often recommended to his devotees: Naam japa (chanting God's name repeatedly) is the best route to attain God in Kaliyug. This method is better than even the *sandhya* adoration or any other sadhana. This is because, resorting to yagnas (oblation offered to the fire god) or following and adhering rigidly to the principles laid by the Vedas and Vedanta is very difficult and painful to the physical body. Therefore, the easiest means is *naam-smaran* (remembering God).

Sai Baba of Shirdi used to advise His devotees and followers to adopt simple and easy methods of attaining self-realization. Although He never instructed any devotee to practise any particular path, mantra, or yoga, but according to the devotee's spiritual inclination, mental attitude, and retention capacity, as well as his family traditions, Baba used to guide him accordingly. Whenever Baba was sitting alone in front of the ever-burning dhuni in Dwarkamayi masjid, and whatever time He spent in Lendibagh (the garden in which Baba used to tend and nurture plants), as well as in the middle of the night, He has been observed by close devotees like Mhalsapati and Tatiya Kote Patil to be repeating God's name to Himself (as mentioned in Shri Sai Satcharita). Chaitanya and his vaishnavite followers used to sing bhajans and do kirtan. Taking Lord's name (Hare Rama Hare Krishna), they would dance in pure ecstasy. Similarly, in Shirdi, during *Takiya* (bhajan and kirtan conducted by Muslim and Sufi devotees), Baba would sing the Lord's name and also dance with devotion and fervour in tune to the bhajans sung by the Sufi devotees. Besides, Baba has always been heard saying *"Allah Malik hai"* implying Allah is Lord and *"Sabka Malik ek"* meaning there is only one Lord.

The life of saints and seers is itself the message they want to communicate to mankind. Time and again, Baba, through His words and actions, used to indicate and remind His devotees that always taking Lord's name or remembering the Sadguru, who is the physical representation of Brahma-Vishnu-Maheswar (the holy trinity) on this earth, is the highest or best form of worship and sadhana. The great saint Tulsidas has explained very beautifully the significance of *Ram naam japa* in Shri Ram Charit Manas. Just like a damsel of heaven who is heavily laden with the most beautiful ornaments, but is not attired with clothes, has no charm, similarly, there is no charm in life without chanting God's name.

Sai Baba was Himself *Sat-Chit-Anand* (pure consciousness, knowledge and bliss personified)) and He used to advise His devotees, *"Have complete faith and trust in your guru since*

*guru is the living God. I do not want any ostentatious show of your
devotion. I am a slave to pure devotion. Whoever pronounces Sai
with pure devotion, I am always there by his side."*

When the elderly lady Radhabai Deshmukh, who had
taken upon Sai Baba as her Param Sadguru, resolved to fast
unto death unless Baba had imparted some mantras to her,
Baba very gently dissuaded her from fasting. He convinced
her that mantras were not important and remembering the
guru was enough to enable a person to traverse the mundane
world. Thus, instead of imparting mantras, Baba advised her,
*"Whoever remembers Me with love and devotion, I shall always
fulfil their desires. Those devotees who wholeheartedly love Me and
talk of My leelas and My life, I shall see to it that they lead a happy
and contented life. One who wholeheartedly surrenders to Me and
meditates with full faith and devotion, I shall give him moksha. This
is My specialty"*

Besides, the omniscient Sainath used to inspire His
devotees to meditate and do *naam japa* (chanting) of one's
Ishtadeva. In this context, the cases of Rao Bahadur Pradhan
and Mrs Khaparde may be cited, which illustrate the
significance of *naam japa.*

Rao Bahadur Pradhan came to know about the divinity
and magnanimity of Sai Baba from Dasganu Maharaj. He
was so much attracted towards Baba that he firmly resolved
to go to Shirdi and take darshan of this great Sadguru. Soon,
he got an opportunity to make a trip to Shirdi. On reaching
Dwarkamayi, he had Baba's darshan, paid his obeisance to
Him, and sat in the darbar. After some time, when the other
devotees had left, Baba gestured him to come closer and
made him sit near Him. At this moment, Baba was humming
a song to himself. Pradhan tried to listen attentively to Baba.
Baba was saying, *"What should we sing? We should sing –
Shri Ram, Jai Ram, Jai Jai Ram."* Hearing this, Pradhan was
overwhelmed and started shedding tears copiously. He, once
again, fell at Baba's feet with a feeling of extreme gratitude.

Later, he explained his actions, saying, "This is exactly what my Kulguru (guru of the dynasty or family) had instructed me to chant. But due to my negligence, I have not been able to carry out my Kulguru's instructions sincerely. Sadguru Sainath, who is the path finder for His devotees, reminded me of my duties and brought me to the right track. This act of Baba brought tears to my eyes and I fell at Baba's feet, wholeheartedly surrendering to Him."

Similarly, when Mrs Khaparde, an ardent devotee of Baba, was massaging Baba's feet in solitude, Baba slowly murmured *"Bolo Raja Ram Raja Ram"* to her. This was the *Shaktipat* (transfer of power) which Baba imparted to Mrs Khaparde, for which she always remained grateful. Baba had explained in very simple words, *"Whoever remembers Me, My attention is always directed towards him. I don't need any conveyance, cart, or carriage to reach him. If he calls Me with love, I reach him within no time."*

*****

17

The Tale of Roti and Onion

The life of saints and seers clearly sends across their message to mankind. Sai Baba, during His sixty years of sojourn in Shirdi, had lived a very simple and unostentatious life. He had told His devotees that one can achieve spiritual bliss by leading a simple and pure life. To achieve God-realization, no paraphernalia, no religious rituals, no austerity measures, and no food restrictions are ever required to be observed. Generally, we believe that those who practise yoga sadhana only consume *satwik* food like fruits. Non-vegetarian food is considered *rajasik* (food that induces action), and spicy food is considered *tamasik* (food that induces sleep or dullness). Some sects, who attach great importance to their dietary habits, consume food devoid of onion and garlic, which are regarded as *tamasik* food. Some people observe Ekadashi fast and do not eat any cereals on Ekadashi day, while some others observe *nirjala* fast (no intake of food or water). However, Sai Baba of Shirdi never approved of such fasts or restrictions in diet. He never attached any importance to dietary regimen. He advised His devotees to observe moderation in food. He gladly accepted His devotees' pure love and devotion. In this context, it is important to cite the incident of roti and onion, which has a large significance in Baba's message.

Once, it so happened that a *sadhak* of yoga visited Shirdi. Though he had gained much knowledge of Yoga Shastra, he had very little practical experience. He had come to Shirdi to take darshan of Baba, as well as to be blessed in his yogic endeavour. When he reached Dwarkamayi, he found Baba sitting in the courtyard of the masjid and eating chapatti and onion. On witnessing this scene, doubts cropped up in his mind. "What kind of Yogeshwar is He? How can this person, eating stale bread with raw onion (onion is a *tamasik* food), remove my deficiency and enable me to be proficient in yoga?" The omniscient Baba could immediately read his thoughts and remarked, "*Oh Nana, he who has the power to digest onion, should eat it and none else.*" Hearing Baba's remark, the yogi was amazed and felt ashamed for doubting Baba's divinity. He fell at Baba's feet with complete surrender and begged for His forgiveness. The ever compassionate Baba then advised the yogi to have control over his thoughts and also not to be perturbed by externalities like food and drinks and thought process. Once this was achieved, it would become easier to practise yoga.

In 1914, during the time of Ramnavami, the holy place of Shirdi was crowded with a large number of devotees. Sai Baba was sitting in front of the scared dhuni, as usual. On this auspicious day, the Muslim devotees celebrated the Urs mela and the Hindu devotees observed the Ramnavami festival simultaneously, with pomp and grandeur. This tradition has been followed in Shirdi since 1912 with Baba's consent and blessings, till today.

An old woman waited outside the masjid for taking Baba's darshan on that day. A large number of devotees had already assembled in the masjid premises with the desire of taking Baba's darshan and being blessed by Him. The old lady was murmuring to herself, "Oh Baba! Please have mercy on this poor, old woman, and give me darshan." Since the place was thronged with thousands and thousands of devotees, no one paid any heed to her pleas in that cacophony. It was almost impossible for her to wade through the crowd to reach the masjid and take Baba's darshan. Fortunately,

Shri Rama Chandra Atmaram Tarkhad, a devotee of Baba, was passing by when his glance fell on the old lady. He was filled with compassion for her on account of her advanced age and sincere devotion. He somehow managed to make his way through the crowd and brought the old woman inside Dwarkamayi. On beholding Baba, the old lady was so overwhelmed that she embraced Baba out of sheer joy. Baba placed His hands on the old woman's head and blessed her. After enquiring about the welfare of her family, He addressed her, "*Mother, I have been waiting for you for a long time. What have you brought for Me?*" She was so touched by Baba's concern that, with tears in her eyes and an emotionally choked voice, she barely managed to say, "Baba, I had brought for you one roti (bread) and two onions. But after walking such a long distance, I felt tired and hungry. So, on the way, I ate half of the roti and one onion near the stream. However, I still have the other half of the roti and one onion, which you can have." Saying these words, the old woman opened the knot at the end of her saree where she had tied the food and handed it to Baba.

Baba accepted the roti and onion very eagerly. After eating it, in a very contended tone, Baba told her, "*Oh mother, I have never eaten such a sweet roti before.*" Hearing Baba's words, the old woman, as well as all those who were present in the darbar, were moved due to Baba's humble gesture. They realized that God and His representatives, in the form of saints and seers, lovingly accept anything when offered with pure love and devotion. Lord Shri Krishna has Himself said in Bhagwad Gita, Chapter IX, "Whosoever offers Me, with love or devotion, a leaf, a flower, a fruit, or water, that offering of love of the pure and self-controlled man is willingly and readily accepted by Me."

When Lord Rama was in exile in the dense forest, a *Shabari* (tribal woman) had offered Him wild fruits out of sheer devotion and love. Lord Rama, without any hesitation at all, had accepted the *Shabari* woman's offering very gladly.

In a similar manner, Sai Baba of Shirdi, who is regarded as Kaliyug's avatar, had gladly accepted the food brought by the old woman with sheer love and devotion. This incident only illustrates the fact that God is a slave of His devotees. In another instance, Baba had not touched (consecrated) the delicacies brought to Him as naivedya in a silver plate by a very affluent lady because the offering had not been made out of pure love and devotion.

*****

18

Atithi Devo Bhavo

In Indian tradition, it is said that *Atithi Devo Bhavo*, which means that a guest is considered as God. But the Sanskrit word "Atithi" represents a guest who comes unannounced, that is, without giving any prior notice regarding the date and time of his arrival. This statement has a special significance in today's material world, where people are too attached to their narrow, selfish desires and possessions. Sai Baba of Shirdi has conveyed the universal truth—*God resides in all beings*—to His devotees through His sayings and numerous actions. Baba wanted that all His devotees should treat every being with equal love and respect.

As per the Shastras, the Brahmins used to observe five yagnas, that is, *Brahma yagna* (offering to Brahmins); *Pitru yagna* (offering to ancestors); *Deva yagna* (offering to God); *Bhoot yagna* (offering to other beings); and *Manushya Atithi yagna* (offering to the guests). Vedas have also instructed that those who treat the guests (guests who come unannounced) with love and affection and serve them with devotion are sure to achieve sadgati. Nanasaheb Chandorkar, who was an orthodox Brahmin, used to offer food and service, according to Vedic instructions, to an unannounced guest every day after the morning puja rituals. He used to anxiously wait for this stranger and would offer food on his arrival. Only after feeding his guest would he take food himself. This was his daily routine. As a Mamlatdar, Deputy Collector, and in other senior positions, he had to tour the remotest parts of his area. Sometimes, when he was away from home, camping in some remote area of his district, he would wait long for a guest, but in vain. This would make Nana think whether the *Vaiswadeva mantra* in the Vedas was correct. He could not get a satisfactory reply and his doubts remained unanswered. After some days, he got a chance to visit Shirdi. The doubts which were there in his mind began to occur again. The antaryami Baba knew what was causing unrest in Nana's mind. Before he could approach Baba with his problems, Baba said, "*Do you think that wherever you go, guests will come to you? But, when guests really come to you, are you able to perceive them?*" Nana could not comprehend the meaning of Baba's words. Baba again said, "*There is nothing wrong in the Vedic principles. You have not deciphered the implications properly. Atithi (guest) here does not imply a Brahmin guest who will visit your house and have food with you. After performing your daily puja in the morning, take some prasad and place it in a corner of your house. This prasad will be gladly enjoyed by several guests. These guests may appear in the form of ants, flies, rats, cats, or dogs. They may not look like guests, but they are, indeed, your guests because God lives in them. So, if you follow this procedure, you will be adhering to the Vedic principles and, in addition, you will be doing yourself good.*" Nana understood well the essence of Baba's words and the true significance of the statement *Atithi Devo Bhavo.*

Baba had explained clearly in simple and lucid language that all living creatures, whether human beings, birds, animals, or insects and flies, feel hungry and if we can appease their hunger in some way, God will be pleased. Sometimes, Baba used to visit the houses of His devotees in different guises just to teach them not to discriminate between the rich and the poor, the low and the high caste, a friend and a stranger, a man and an animal or insect, and to treat every guest equally, with love and affection.

Once Mhalsapati, a great devotee of Baba, was having his midday meal when a sick looking dog started barking in front of his house. Mhalsapati, instead of giving some food to the dog, hit it with a stick, causing more pain and injury to the animal. That evening, when the devotees assembled in the darbar at Dwarkamayi, they were shocked to see stick marks on Baba's back. When enquired, Baba looked towards Mhalsapati and said, *"I had gone to his house to beg for some food. In return, I was beaten and injured."* Mhalsapati hung his head in utter shame.

The first shloka of Isha Upanishad establishes the supreme universal truth. The axiom states, *"Ishavashyam Idam Sarvam, Jatkinchit Jagatyam Jagat,"* which means that God pervades in every creature and in the entire universe. This axiom should be realized by every devotee and he should love and care for everyone in this universe, because there is no difference between one entity and another. This was what Baba desired for His devotees to follow. He has mentioned, time and again, while sitting in His darbar at Dwarkamayi masjid, to His dear devotees, *"Never drive away your guest. Nobody is a stranger. Know this that, whoever comes to you, has come because of his "rinanubandh"* (meaning drawn by past ties). *Therefore, treat him with love and affection and try to help him as per your ability. That is real humaneness."*

Another ardent devotee of Baba, Shri Upasani Maharaj, during his stay in Shirdi, would prepare naivedya for Baba. One day, after preparing food for naivedya, he carried it to Dwarkamayi. On the way, he met a hungry dog. However, Upasani Maharaj felt that the auspicious food was meant for consecration by Baba and not meant for an insignificant creature like a dog. Later, when he presented the naivedya before Baba, he was reprimanded by Him. *"When I had come to you for food, you refused to give me any Why are you offering me now?"* Upasani failed to understand the meaning of Baba's words. Then Baba explained that the hungry dog was none other than He Himself. Upasani realized his mistake and resolved not to repeat it. The next day, after preparing naivedya, he waited anxiously for the dog's arrival. However, there was no sign of the dog. So, with a heavy heart, he carried the naivedya to Dwarkamayi. At Dwarkamayi, he found a sickly and diseased Sudra (low caste) person standing near the wall. Upasani Maharaj was a high caste Brahmin and he was annoyed at the sight of the Sudra person because he was carrying the sacred naivedya for Baba. He told him in an irritated tone to go away. Later, when he came inside Dwarkamayi, Baba told him, *"Yesterday you did not give Me any food. Today you have driven Me away. I will not accept your naivedya."*

Upasani Maharaj was surprised to hear this from Baba. In a shocked tone, he asked, "Baba, were you that sickly and diseased Sudra?" In response, Baba explained to Upasani in a simple way, *"What do you think, am I confined to three and half cubits of body? I pervade everywhere and in every being. When you will recognize Me in every being, then only you will recognize My true self."*

Baba had transformed Upasani from an ordinary person to a Sadguru and this was a lesson on *atithi satkar* (treating your guest well) imparted to Upasani during the transformation process. This is also a lesson for every devotee that God exists in every being and therefore we should love and respect one another.

*****

19

Amraleela

Since ages, incarnations of God have manifested on this earth and through their incredible leelas they have displayed their divinity. Sai Baba of Shirdi, the Param Sadguru and the living incarnation of Brahma, Vishnu, and Maheswar in Kaliyug, has also exhibited several extraordinary leelas to inspire His devotees and motivate them towards the path of truth and righteousness. Sai Baba is our *bhukti-mukti data* because He takes care of the pains, anguish, and problems of His devotees and fulfils both their materialistic as well as spiritual desires. In this context, *amraleela* or the mango miracle can be cited to show how Baba fulfilled the desire of His devotee Damu Anna, the lesson taught to him, as well as the message Baba sends across to His dear devotees.

Damodar Sawalram Rasne was an ardent devotee of Baba. He was an affluent businessman, based at Ahmednagar. Baba used to fondly address him as Damu Anna. Being a prosperous businessman, he had amassed a lot of wealth and property. However, nature had not been kind to him and he was deprived of the joy of fathering a child. When his first wife failed to give him a child, he got married for the second time. However, he met with the same fate in case of his second wife also. He consulted several astrologers and found out that because of inauspicious planetary positions in his horoscope, there was no prospect of any child in his life. This revelation made him sad and he lost his peace of mind. However, he had full faith in his benevolent Sai. So he decided to seek Baba's blessings to get a child.

In the meantime, the Mamlatdar of Goa, Shri Rale, had sent a package containing three hundred mangoes to Sai Baba. All the mangoes were in good condition. However, Baba kept only eight mangoes and instructed Shama to distribute the rest. There were some children playing in the courtyard of the masjid. Baba was very fond of them. When the children came and picked four out of the eight mangoes, Baba expressed His annoyance. He said, "*These mangoes are meant for Damu Anna, so don't take them away.*" The children then informed Baba that Damu Anna had not arrived in Shirdi. The omniscient Baba replied, "*Damu is coming.*" True to Baba's words and to the utter surprise of all present, after two hours Damu Anna entered Dwarkamayi and came to Baba to pay his obeisance. Baba handed over four mangoes to Damu Anna and said, "*Take, eat these mangoes and die.*" Damu Anna was taken aback to hear such words from Baba. He had come to Baba to seek His blessings for a child with a lot of hope and aspiration. However, here was Baba telling him to eat the mangoes and then die. He wondered whether Baba was blessing him or cursing him. Mhalsapati, another devotee of Baba, who was sitting close by explained to Damu Anna the significance of Baba's words. The attachment, allurement, and delusion in this material world create an illusion which can be compared to death. By death, Baba meant death of ego and to shed one's ego at Baba's feet is indeed true bliss. How fortunate is the devotee who Baba blesses in such a manner!

The highly knowledgeable saint, Sanat Kumar, has remarked in this context that the allurement for this materialistic world (life-death bondage) is an illusion and creates a delusion which can be regarded as synonymous to death. In a similar manner, although the all-knowing Sai Baba blessed Damu Anna with children and fulfilled his desire, He also forewarned him that by getting children Damu Anna shall be enveloped by maya (illusory world).

Then Baba, in a softer tone, addressed Damu Anna. He said, "*Do not eat yourself, but give them to your younger wife. This Amraleela* (miracle of mangoes) *will give her four sons and four daughters.*" In due course of time, Baba's blessings proved correct and the astrologers' predictions turned out to be wrong.

This incident shows that the blessings of saints and seers always bear fruit. The efficacy and greatness of Baba's words have been exhibited when Baba was in His physical form. However, His divinity continues to prevail even after several years of His mahasamadhi in 1918. Baba had told His devotees, "*Believe Me, though I pass away, My bones in My tomb would be speaking, moving, and communicating with those who would surrender themselves wholeheartedly to Me. Do not be anxious that I would be absent from you. You will hear My bones speaking and discussing your welfare. But remember Me always, believe in Me heart and soul, and then you will be most benefitted.*"

Many devotees who have wholeheartedly surrendered to Baba believe that if a person prays with devotion and faith, his prayers are answered without fail and the devotee receives kind assurance from the Samadhi. Once Damu Anna, while massaging Baba's feet, looked at Baba's frail physique and deteriorating health and wondered, "If Baba were to pass away, I would become an orphan and would lose my place of shelter for ever. How will I fare then?" But Baba immediately removed this fear from his mind and answered his unasked question. Baba said, "*There is no need to be perturbed at the thought that I will not be there with you in the future. I shall always remain active and vigorous from My Samadhi. I shall be there whenever and wherever you need Me.*"

Baba took mahasamadhi in 1918. In 1936, Damu Anna has been recorded to have said to Narasimha Swami, "Baba is still there with me and has been guiding me all the time, even after taking mahasamadhi." Not only Damu Anna, but lakhs and lakhs of devotees who have wholeheartedly surrendered to

Baba, experience Baba's guidance and blessings in their hour of need even today. They also firmly believe that whoever sets his feet on the holy soil of Shirdi or climbs the stairs of Dwarkamayi, all his grief, pain, miseries, and anguish will vanish instantaneously. Although Baba is no longer in His mortal coil, more and more devotees are visiting Shirdi and paying their heartfelt obeisance to Baba's Samadhi in the Samadhi Mandir.

*****

20

Symbol of Modesty

Shirdi, a small non-descript village in Kopergaon Taluk of Ahmednagar district in Maharashtra, rose to prominence and limelight only because Baba had chosen it as his *karam bhumi*. When Baba was in His mortal coil, He spent over sixty years in Shirdi, which was His abode. At Shirdi, Baba was the focal point for all the rustic village folks. He was their companion as well as guide, navigating them through tough problems, bailing them out of difficult situations and rescuing them from all kinds of evils and afflictions.

Once a fakir called Javhar Ali visited Shirdi and started living in the masjid. The fakir was learned, knew the Quran by heart, and had a sweet tongue. The simple folks of Shirdi were impressed by his discourses on the Quran. By and by, he started treating Baba as his disciple and made Baba do all his errands. Baba did not mind being treated in this way and gladly served Javhar Ali. Javhar Ali was not aware of either the divinity or the supreme attributes of this Godly incarnation. Baba, however, never objected and served him dutifully and sincerely. Although the guru was not aware of his disciple's worth, the disciple was well aware of the shortcomings of His guru. Then Javhar Ali decided to go to Rahata. So he took his disciple, Sai Baba, along with him. The loving devotees of Baba in Shirdi did not like that Baba should stay away from them, in Rahata. So they went in a delegation to bring Him back. They met Baba and told Him the purpose of their visit. Baba, on hearing this, warned them that Javhar

Ali was an ill-tempered, angry fellow and he would not permit Him to leave Rahata. So Baba dissuaded them and advised them to go back to Shirdi and not to confront the obstinate fakir. While they were thus discussing, the fakir turned up. When he found that they were trying to take away his disciple, he became wild with anger. There were some heated arguments and it was finally decided that both the guru and the disciple should return to Shirdi. Accordingly, they came back to Shirdi and lived there.

The saints and seers who visited Shirdi, knowing the worth of Sai Baba, would come to pay their regard to Him, even though, at that time, Baba was very young. Among the saints, two renowned and acknowledged saints were Devi Das and Janaki Das. They were, in fact, followers of the bhakti marg. They held Baba in high esteem. They often used to discuss complex issues with Baba since Baba always had a solution for every problem. As the saying goes, "The goldsmith knows the worth of gold," similarly, these saints knew the true worth of Sadguru Sainath and considered Him as a precious diamond amid a heap of cow dung. Therefore, they had also become disciples of Baba. They did not approve of Baba serving the fraud fakir, Javhar Ali. They got agitated at the sight of the fakir throwing tantrums on Baba, who was an embodiment of humility and modesty. And so Devidas, at an appropriate opportunity, challenged Javhar Ali for a debate in the presence of the people of Shirdi. In the debate, Javhar Ali lost to Devidas. In utter disgrace, Javhar Ali had to flee from Shirdi and take refuge in Bijapur. After several years, he returned to Shirdi and prostrated before Sai Baba, with true repentance. The delusion, that he was the guru and Sai Baba was his disciple, had been cleared. On the other hand, Baba treated him with love and respect. This incident shows the modesty and humility of Baba. This was the message Baba wanted to convey to His dear devotees. Baba, by His actual conduct, showed how one should get rid of ego in order to attain the highest end, that is, self-realization.

Nanavali, a devotee of Baba, was known for his peculiar behaviour. He would get agitated and then scold and abuse all who were around. However, he was a sincere devotee of Baba and served Him with a lot of devotion and dedication. Once, he had a strange thought in his mind. He thought that the seat on which Baba sat was the seat of power. So, if he could sit on the seat, he would also command the same amount of love and respect as Baba. One day, all of a sudden, he approached Baba, who was seated on His gaddi (seat), and asked Him to vacate the gaddi for him. Baba, without any protest, coolly got up from His seat and allowed Nanavali to occupy it. After being seated on the gaddi for some time, Nanavali, on his own, got up and requested Baba to occupy the gaddi. Then he fell at Baba's feet and begged for His forgiveness. However, Baba was not perturbed even the slightest, with Nanavali's strange behaviour. Rather, when the devotees present in the darbar expressed their annoyance at Nanavali's unbecoming behaviour, Baba advised them to face the situation with patience(saburi). What exemplary modesty Baba has exhibited!

Just like a fertile tree laden with fruit bends with their weight, similarly, a knowledgeable person is always humble. Sai Baba was a repository of knowledge and a personification of modesty and humility. He never considered Himself as a Sadguru. He used to, very humbly, say, "*I am a slave of My devotees. Due to the mercy of Allah, I have been able to dedicate Myself in your service. For this, I am ever grateful.*" This statement of Baba is a reflection of His modesty and humility.

*****

21

Sai Sagun Upasana

Upasana (worship) are of two types — *nirgun* (unmanifested) upasana and *sagun* (manifested) upasana. Nirgun is formless while the sagun is with form. However, both denote the same Brahma. Some prefer to worship the nirgun Brahma while others prefer to worship the sagun Brahma. The great saint, Sant Tulsi Das, has mentioned in Shri Ram Charit Manas that there is no subtle difference between nirgun and sagun form of worship. Both forms enable us to cross this mundane world of existence, which is intricately cobwebbed by the strings of maya (illusion).

According to Chapter XII of Gita, sagun upasana is simple and free from complexities. Human beings are endowed with a physical body in which all the *indriyas* are located. Therefore, it is easier on the part of a human being to concentrate on a manifested form of God and offer his worship to that form. Nirgun upasana is a more difficult path to follow since it requires the follower to give up all kinds of vices before taking up spiritual training. Therefore, a person can follow sagun upasana for a while in order to enhance his faith and devotion. Then, the progression from sagun to nirgun upasana becomes easier and follows naturally. Baba has always advocated two golden virtues — shradha and saburi — to be adopted by every devotee for his spiritual development. Sai Baba has advised His devotees to incorporate these twin principles in their daily life. A devotee can follow any spiritual path, like remembering or meditating on either his spiritual guru or Ishtadeva. Baba, in the course of His conversations, has also conveyed to His devotees that only guru should be worshipped, because guru is God. When an elderly lady devotee, Smt. Radhabai Deshmukh, undertook a fast unto death at Shirdi, Baba had come to her rescue. Baba very kindly spoke to her, "*You may attain Parmartha (self-realization) if you remember Me and My swarup (physical appearance) with devotion.*" Baba has also assured some of His devotees, "*I am indebted to whoever remembers Me with love and devotion.*" Even in Gita, Shri Krishna Bhagwan spoke in a similar tone, "Those who carry out My upasana (worship) with great devotion and their entire mind and soul is dedicated to Me, he is the best yogi (sadhak) according to Me."

Upasana literally implies taking a seat next to someone or sitting in close proximity. However, spiritually, upasana refers to abiding by your guru's instructions, concentrating on your ideals and, in the process, moving closer to your goals. This is what the scriptures have recommended. A devotee usually starts his sadhana by worshipping God's idol or portrait. Slowly and gradually, he starts worshipping the divine consciousness in his inner self. Eventually, he gets immersed in the nirgun Brahma (formless divinity). Shri Ramakrishna Paramhansa, who is regarded as an incarnation of God, has explained in very simple and lucid language that God, Bhagwad (Vedas, Shastras, and Puranas) and the devotee constitute one entity. This entity symbolizes the holy trinity. Just like water gets converted into ice or vapour depending upon the surrounding temperature conditions, in a similar manner, in the first stage, a child starts crawling before he is capable of walking. In the second stage, the child tries to walk with support and, eventually, in the final stage becomes capable of walking without any support. So Shri Ramakrishna Paramhansa has advised all devotees to recognize God in whatever form they can behold. It is the divine love which is of prime import rather than the idol of God or His portrait. Eventually, the worshipper sees no difference between himself and God because his wholehearted devotion unites him with God. The experience is the same despite whatever path (sagun or nirgun) a devotee may follow to reach the goal. The ultimate goal is to become an inseparable part of God Himself.

Sai Baba, an incarnation of God, had taken a mortal body and had descended on this earth to relieve the sufferings of mankind. He was *Stithapragyan*, as He was totally detached and indifferent to His surroundings. He was neither elated by pleasures nor depressed by misfortunes. However, His heart would melt at the sufferings of His devotees. There are numerous instances when He has taken the sufferings of His devotees upon Himself. According to Hemadpant, the author of Shri Sai Satcharita, the most effective path to attain our object, that is, self-realization, is to surrender ourselves to a Sadguru who has himself attained God-realization. What cannot be achieved by studying religious texts or participating in religious discourses can be easily achieved with the blessings of a Sadguru. Just as the sun gives light, which all the stars put together cannot do, so also the Sadguru alone can impart spiritual wisdom, which all the sacred books and sermons cannot do. A Sadguru is an epitome of all the virtues—forgiveness, calmness, disinterestedness, charity, benevolence, control of mind and body, egolessness, and so on. Sai Baba of Shirdi was such a Sadguru and an embodiment of all these virtues. He loved all beings because He perceived God and divinity in them. Hence, the devotees have lodged in their hearts the image of this detached fakir, the blissful Sainath.

Baba used to respect the devotees' faith and devotion and used to allow them to worship according to their desire. According to Him, "*Jayaman Jaisa bhava, taya taisa anubhava*," which means that whatever is the faith and devotion of a person, he will have an experience accordingly.

Once, a friend of Tatya Saheb Noolkar (a devotee of Baba), named Dr Pandit arrived in Shirdi for Baba's darshan. After paying his obeisance to Baba, he sat quietly in a corner of the masjid and watched the activities going on in the darbar. Dadabhat, a dear devotee of Baba, was then offering puja-archana to Baba. Suddenly, on an impulse, Dr Pandit got up from his seat and took the puja thali (plate containing puja material) from Dadabhat. Then, taking some sandal paste from the plate, drew a *tripundarekha* (three horizontal lines) on Baba's forehead. Everybody was surprised to find Baba remaining calm, instead of reprimanding Dr Pandit. Driven by curiosity, Dadabhat asked Baba, "How is it that, though you object to the sandal paste being applied by others to Your forehead, You allowed Dr Pandit to do so?" Baba replied that Dr Pandit believed Him to be the same as his guru, Raghunath Maharaj of Dhopeshwar. Therefore, he had applied the sandal paste to His forehead as he would have done to His guru. This was the reason why Baba did not object to Dr Pandit's impulsive act. On enquiry, Dr Pandit confirmed this and said that this was his exact feeling.

In another incident, Mule Shastri of Nasik, who was an orthodox Agnihotri Brahmin, once came to Shirdi to meet Bapusaheb Buti, the famous millionaire of Nagpur, who later constructed the Samadhi Mandir of Baba. After meeting him, he accompanied Buti to the masjid for Baba's darshan. Inside the masjid, Mule Shastri was awestruck to behold his own beloved guru, Gholap Swami sitting there in Baba's place. He wondered if it was a dream. Ultimately, leaving aside all doubts, he fell at his guru's feet realizing that both his guru and Baba were the same. Many other devotees have also experienced and visualized their own guru in Baba. Some devotees have even seen their Ishtadeva in Sai Baba.

Lord Shri Krishna has aptly stated, "Saints are My soul personified. They are My living forms."

*****

22

Sabka Malik Ek

Saints are the representatives of God on earth. Divine souls descend on this earth with a mission. They remain indifferent to worldly matters and lead a serene and peaceful life, dedicating themselves to relieve the sufferings of mankind and working for the welfare of the society. Indeed, they work with a missionary zeal, without any vested interest or any expectation of results. Sai Baba of Shirdi, the Param Sadguru, had assumed a human body, but His deeds testified to His Godhood. Indeed, He is *Sat-Chit-Anand*. He was always engrossed in the Almighty Lord and was always heard saying, *"Sab Allah hi Allah hai. Har sab Allah Miah Cha ahe"*. The meaning of this is that the Lord or Allah is all pervasive. Everything in this universe belongs to Him.

The saints and seers manifest their divinity through their exemplary good conduct, propriety, and righteousness. Shri Ramakrishna Paramhansa had once explained to a disciple in a very simple way, "Brass utensils should always be cleaned to retain their polish and lustre. Similarly, saints should always engage themselves in religious discourses, *naam japa*, and singing bhajans and kirtans about the glory of the Lord. All these enable the cleansing of the body, mind, and soul. Therefore, what is of import is meditation and contemplation on the Almighty Lord."

Sai Baba has often been heard remarking, *"Sabka Malik ek. Ham kisike bande nahin hai, Allah ke bande hain."* This means that

God is the sole owner and we are His children. Once, Baba shifted His base from Shirdi (His *karam bhumi*) to Rahata. He started living there with another fakir, much to the chagrin of His devotees. Rahata was only four kilometres away from Shirdi. Many of His close devotees used to travel to Rahata often to take Baba's darshan, as well as to take His advice in their matters. Once, a youth visited Rahata to call on his friend for financial assistance. Before visiting his friend, he went for Baba's darshan. When Baba enquired about his welfare, the youth narrated about his impending marriage and the purpose of his visit to Rahata. The omniscient Baba smiled and remarked, "*Who is yours? Who gives and who takes?*" The youth was bewildered at Baba's remark and could not understand it. Then Baba reassured him saying, "*Allah Malik hai. Your finances will be arranged and so you need not worry on that account.*" The young man, after prostrating in front of Baba, left for his friend's house.

When he met his friend, he requested him to lend him two thousand rupees as a loan for his marriage expenses. However, his friend declined to give him any money. Disheartened, he left his friend's house. On the way back, he met an acquaintance. Concerned at his pitiful demeanour, the acquaintance asked him the reason for his worries. At that time, a moneylender was passing by. It so happened that the acquaintance knew the moneylender very well. So he requested him to lend the requisite amount and also requested him not to charge a high rate of interest because of his friend's financial constraints. Surprisingly, the moneylender immediately lent him the amount and also waived off the interest. The young man felt greatly relieved and happy that his financial problem had been sorted out. Filled with gratitude, he remembered Baba's parting words. He then realized the significance of what Baba had said.

The essence is God is the only rescuer in this universe. In times of adversity and calamity, it is God who bails us out. The entire universe belongs to God and He is the wire puller.

The world is dependent on Him and no one is independent. He is the only giver and we are all receivers. He controls the entire universe and all beings obey His commands.

*****

23

All-Pervasive Sai Baba

As per the Shastras and other religious texts, the Almighty Lord is omniscient, omnipresent, and omnipotent. Even Lord Shri Krishna has mentioned in the fifth chapter of Gita, *"I enjoy the fruits of all penance and sacrifice. I am the God on earth and the friend of all. Whoever realizes this truth will attain peace and happiness in life."*

There are many incidents which have happened when Baba was in His mortal coil at Shirdi, and even after Baba's mahasamadhi, which provide evidence to the fact that Baba is all-pervasive. Many incredible leelas have occurred during Baba's presence, which stand testimony to the fact that Baba is undoubtedly omnipresent. Shri Ram Chandra Atmaram Tarkhad and his family, who hailed from Bandra, Mumbai, were ardent devotees of Baba. Once, Smt. Tarkhad and her son wished to spend the summer vacation at Shirdi. However, they had an apprehension that the daily puja of Baba and offering of naivedya in their house at Bandra would get interrupted due to their absence. Shri Tarkhad, who was watching their hesitation and reluctance, reassured them that he would perform Baba's puja every day, as well as offer the naivedya, without fail. Therefore, both mother and son could proceed to Shirdi without any doubt in their minds. So Smt. Tarkhad and her son left for Shirdi, tension-free, and began to spend their holidays very happily in the holy company of Sai Baba.

One day, when Smt. Tarkhad and her son came to Dwarkamayi for Baba's darshan, they were shocked to hear from Baba, "*I had gone to your house in Bandra, but I found all the doors locked. Somehow I managed to get inside. However, since there was nothing for Me to eat in your house, I have returned unappeased.*" Shri Tarkhad's son immediately understood that his father must have forgotten to offer naivedya that day to Baba. So he sought Baba's permission to return to their home, without further delay. Looking at the perturbed boy, the merciful Baba, in a tone full of love and compassion, spoke to him, "*There is nothing to be worried in this matter. You can offer Me naivedya here.*" Abiding by Baba's instructions, the son dropped the idea of returning to Bandra. Instead, he wrote a letter to his father about the whole matter as narrated by Baba. At Bandra, Shri Tarkhad had also realized his serious lapse. That he had forgotten to offer naivedya to Baba, made him feel guilty. Filled with remorse, he wrote an apology, addressed to Baba. Both father and son received their respective letters on the same day. In this incident, Baba has illustrated that whoever remembers Him with love and devotion or offers any naivedya with faith, is accepted by Him, without fail.

In 1918, Gulbe Shastri had gone to Shirdi for Baba's darshan. He had carried with him holy water of Ganges and performed *abhisekh* (holy bath) of Baba with the *Gangajal*. Later, he sought Baba's permission to go to Sajjangad to observe the Ramnavami festival. Then Baba had, very briefly, said, "*I am here and I am also there.*" Later, Gulbe Shastri departed for Sajjangad. On reaching Sajjangad, his joy knew no bounds when he found his Sainath, instead of the deity, Shri Rama. The significance of Baba's words "*I am here and I am also there*" soon dawned on him. He realized the universal truth that Baba was omnipresent. Brimming with love and devotion for his Sainath, he bowed down in prostration at the feet of the Lord. As he got up, he found Baba nowhere.

There are more leelas of Baba which reveal the truth that Baba resides in every living creature, because Baba is one with them. This axiomatic truth was conveyed by none other than Baba to His dear devotee, Smt. Tarkhad, in two separate incidents during her sojourn at Shirdi. One afternoon, when Smt. Tarkhad was about to have her mid-day meal, she found a dog barking very pitifully in front of her house. Smt. Tarkhad took one chapatti from her plate and gave it to the hungry dog. The dog happily ate the bread. Sometime later, a pig covered with mud and filth all over its body arrived at her doorstep. Smt. Tarkhad gave some food to the pig also. She had fed both the animals out of her kindness and so had not attached any importance to the incidents. However, when she arrived at the masjid for Baba's darshan later in the afternoon, she was gladly welcomed by Baba. Baba addressed her and said, "*Mother, I was hungry and you have fed Me sumptuously and My famished pranas* (life forces) *have been satisfied. Always act like this and this will stand you in good stead. Serving food to the hungry is the greatest charity one can perform and therefore the most meritorious service.*" Smt. Tarkhad, however, could not comprehend the meaning of Baba's words. She asked Baba, "When did I serve you food? I am dependent on others, here in Shirdi and when did you come to my house, for I have not seen you anywhere near my house."

Baba explained to Smt. Tarkhad that by serving the two hungry animals (the dog and the pig) with food, she had served none other than Baba Himself. By appeasing their hunger, she had satisfied Baba's pranas. This statement of Baba signifies that He is one with all living creatures. If we perceive this divine truth that God pervades everywhere and if we see God in all beings, then we can serve everyone with love and affection. Because, Baba has said, "*He who sees Me in all living creatures, is My beloved.*"

Another dear devotee of Baba, Prof. Narke, has mentioned from his personal experience, "Whoever has observed Baba in minute detail and has studied seriously about Him, can realize the divinity of this great soul. He can realize that Baba is not confined to a body of three and a half cubits, but is formless, as He pervades the entire universe."

Sometimes, Baba would narrate incidents of past lives of people while sitting before the dhuni, which would baffle the listeners. He would relate details of incidents that had happened in the lives of His devotees residing far away from Shirdi and how He had come to their rescue. He would even go to the extent of describing the past and future lives of some of His devotees and even birds and animals. Baba had once told His devotees about His omnipresence. He said, *"Wherever you are, whatever you do or say, remember that I am hearing and knowing everything. I require no conveyance, carriage, or transport, because I pervade everywhere."*

*****

24

Omniscient Sai Baba

In *Vishnu Sahashranaam,* the divinity of God has been vividly described as "*Sarvangya Sarvatomukha,*" which means one who knows everything and every being in its entirety, and one who is looking in every direction. Sai Baba is the incarnation of God. Although He has spent a large part of His life in a small and tiny village called Shirdi, He was well aware of what was happening at other places, far away from Shirdi. He could also anticipate the misfortune or troubles which would befall on His dear devotees. There are many incidents which provide ample testimony to the fact that Baba is omniscient and describe how Baba has come to the rescue of His dear devotees, who lived in places far away from Shirdi, when they were in grave danger and trouble. Strange were the ways how Baba rescued them, even when He was in Shirdi. Also, His devotees at far off places would get answers to their queries, even though Baba would not be physically present at that place.

Once, Baba was sitting in His darbar at Dwarkamayi masjid with His devotees, when He suddenly said, "*My Nana is very thirsty. Shouldn't we quench his thirst?*" At that very moment, forty miles away from Shirdi, in the Harishchandra hills, Baba's devotee, Nanasaheb Chandorkar, braving the scorching heat of peak summer, was climbing up for darshan of the deity at the hilltop. Nanasaheb was then the Deputy Collector of Ahmednagar. When he had traversed half of the journey, he felt very thirsty. His mouth was parched and he felt weak. However, none of the staff who was accompanying him had water with them. Nana remembered his Baba and said, "If my Baba was here, He would have definitely slaked my thirst." However, his companions, on hearing his remark, said, "Baba is not here. So, what is the benefit of remembering him? Rather, you should try to climb the hills with patience in order to reach your destination." But, Nanasaheb, who felt very weak due to the thirst and heat, was unable to take a step further and sat down upon a big boulder lying on the path. Soon, a bhil (a hill tribal) carrying firewood on his head appeared before Nana. Nanasaheb asked the bhil very politely, "Can I get some water to drink? " The bhil replied, "There is water below the very boulder on which you are sitting," and disappeared. Nana's staff immediately set upon the task of removing the huge boulder from its position. When they moved the boulder, they found that the bhil was absolutely correct. True to his words, fresh and clean water was found underneath the boulder. Nana was able to quench his thirst and continued his journey with renewed vigour.

Some days later, when Nana visited Shirdi and went to Dwarkamayi for Baba's darshan, Baba asked him *"Nana when you were very thirsty I had provided you with water."* Hearing Baba's statement, Nanasaheb was astounded and realized that the bhil was, in reality, the omnipresent Baba, who had come to his rescue and had saved him from thirst.

The past, present and future were never hidden from Sai Baba. Baba knew the past lives of His devotees and could also anticipate what was going to happen in the future. In April 1913, Professor G. Narke visited Shirdi to take Baba's darshan. He was ushered inside Dwarkamayi by Shama, a close devotee of Baba. When Shama tried to introduce Prof. Narke to Baba, Baba, in a very candid tone said, *"You are introducing him to Me. I know him for thirty generations."* Narke was awestruck to hear Baba's remark. This was his first visit to Shirdi and the incidents thereafter, which took place in quick succession, removed all doubts and questions from his mind.

At noon aarti time, without any reason, Baba started screaming loudly, as if He was scolding somebody. But nobody knew why Baba was so agitated. Narke, who was watching everything, thought to himself, "Is Baba mad?" But he remained quiet and did not share his thoughts with anyone. When the aarti was over, he left for the wada. When Narke visited Dwarkamayi later in the afternoon, Baba addressed him in a very soft and loving voice and said, "*Narke, I am not mad. Can a mother be annoyed with her children? Does the sea return all the water of different rivers which have flown into its bed?*" Narke then understood that no thoughts were hidden from Baba. He realized that Baba was omniscient and had all the qualities of a Sadguru. Baba was the manifestation of God on earth.

It has been observed that many times the guru chooses his own disciples. Param Sadguru Sai Baba was the master of *Ritambar Pragya*. The past, present, and future were all known to Sai Baba. Baba was aware of the fact that Nanasaheb Chandorkar was His disciple for the last four generations. Therefore, He re-established His relationship with Nana in order to guide him and ensure his self-realization. At that time, Nanasaheb was a highly placed officer in the Revenue Department of the Government. Despite Nana's position and status, Baba did not hesitate to send him an invitation to meet through Kulkarni, a junior level Government servant. At first, Nana was surprised to receive such an invitation from an unknown fakir and so ignored it. However, after receiving three such persistent invitations, he could not suppress his curiosity and went to meet Baba. On reaching Shirdi and paying his obeisance to Baba, he asked Him the reason why he was called to Shirdi. Baba was very straightforward in his reply. He said, "*I wanted to renew our relationship, which has been existing for the last four generations. This rinanubandh* (debt from the past ties) *has been responsible to bring you here to*

Shirdi." Gradually, in the company of Baba, Nanasaheb could realize His greatness. Several incidents which happened in his life and the way Baba came to his rescue only increased his faith in Him. He accepted Baba as his Guru and God and surrendered himself completely to Him.

Once, when Nanasaheb was posted and residing in Kalyan, a beggar woman visited his house to beg for alms. Nana's wife gave her some *bhajni* (a kind of fried rice). But, the beggar woman was not satisfied with what she had received. She kept on asking for more. Nana's wife got agitated with her and reported the matter to Nana. Nana also got angry with the woman's insistence for more alms and shouted at her, "Go away immediately, otherwise I will ask the *darwan* (security personnel) to drive you away." The beggar woman got scared and disappeared. In course of time, Nana forgot this incident. However, the omniscient Baba, sitting at Dwarkamayi in distant Shirdi, monitored the activities of His devotees very minutely. Several days passed and when Nana visited Shirdi again, Baba kept quiet and did not enquire about his welfare. Nana was very disturbed at this behaviour. When he asked Baba about His indifferent behaviour, Baba replied, "*After remaining in contact with Me for such a long time, your behaviour was totally unwanted and uncalled for. If you did not want to give more bhajni to the beggar woman, you could have politely refused her. Why did you have to threaten and exhibit your power in front of the poor woman? Such behaviour is unbecoming of you.*" Nana was aghast and stunned to hear this from Baba. He could say nothing in his defence. He realized that Baba was aware of even the slightest mistake committed by His devotees. Most importantly, He made tireless and relentless efforts to rectify their faults and put His devotees on the right track, that is, the track of righteousness.

*****

25

Navadha Bhakti

There are several paths or recourses to realize God, such as, Karma Yoga, Gyan Yoga, japa, tapa, study of religious scriptures, and so on. Although these methods are very effective and good, the bhakti marg is the easiest way to realize God. This is evident from Shri Ram Charit Manas, written by the great saint, Sant Tulsi Das, in which Lord Shri Rama has told a tribal woman (a true devotee of Lord Rama) as follows: "A person who has the good fortune of hailing from a good family, dynasty, religion, caste, and creed, but devoid of any devotion, can be compared to clouds devoid of water vapour and, therefore, is futile. I only recognize the devotion of My devotees." Similarly, Param Sadguru Shri Sai Baba was an admirer of the bhakti marg. In His opinion, unflinching devotion, firm faith, and constant patience enable the grace of Guru and God. According to Baba, "*I am always with him who remembers Me with devotion and considers himself as one with Me. I am a bond-slave of My devotees.*"

This unflinching devotion is the best kind of love for one's Guru or God. Being immersed in such pure love, Meerabai, a devotee of Lord Krishna), had sung from the core of her heart, "*Mere to Giridhar Gopal doosra na koi*". This means that I only consider Girihdar Gopal, another name of Lord Krishna, as my Lord and no one else. To instill this unflinching love and devotion in our hearts, Baba has mentioned about the *Navadha Bhakti* (nine-fold path of devotion).

Once, a gentleman called Anantrao Patankar from Pune visited Shirdi to take Baba's darshan. On reaching Shirdi, he offered his obeisance to Baba and said, "I have studied the Vedas, Vedanta, Upanishads, and other religious scriptures. I have heard the Puranas, but still I have not gained mental peace. If the mind is not calm, all the knowledge attained is in vain. I have heard that by Your kind words and a mere glance, You have showered bliss on many persons. So take pity on me and kindly shower Your blessings on me." Baba then narrated a parable in order to explain to him the contents of *Navadha Bhakti*. He said, "*Once a merchant had come to Shirdi. His only desire was to attain the grace of Guru or God. A mare passed nine balls of stool in front of this merchant. The merchant, a devout seeker, spread his dhoti to gather all the nine balls in it. In the process he attained peace.*"

Patankar was unable to comprehend the meaning of this parable. He, therefore, approached Dada Kelkar to explain the meaning. Dada Kelkar was a very close devotee of Baba and had stayed in Baba's company for a long time. He replied, "I, too, do not understand all that Baba says and means. However, at His inspiration, I shall tell you whatever I have come to understand. The mare is God's grace and the nine balls of stool are the nine forms of bhakti. They are as follows: (i) *Shravan* (hearing); (ii) *Kirtan* (praying); (iii) *Smaran* (remembering); (iv) *Padasevan* (resorting to the feet); (v) *Archan* (worship); (vi) *Namaskar* (bowing); (vii) *Dasya* (service); (viii) *Sakhyam* (friendship); (ix) *Atmanivedan* (surrender of the self). If any of these is faithfully pursued, God will be pleased and manifest Himself before the devotee. All the sadhanas like japa (vocal worship), tapa (penance), yoga practice, studying the scriptures, and so on, are of no use, unless they are done with devotion. Knowledge of the Vedas, mastery over the scriptures, or the knowledge attained over time, are of no avail. What is required is full devotion. Consider yourself as a seeker of truth and try to cultivate the nine-fold devotion with sincerity and enthusiasm. Then you will attain peace of mind and composure."

One of the foremost devotees of Lord Vishnu, Prahlad, had spoken about the nine-fold devotion as follows:

(i) *Shravan* means listening to the discourses of saints and seers, reading religious scriptures, or listening to the glory of God.

(ii) *Kirtan* means that the devotee himself is involved in chanting the name of the Lord. Chaitanya Mahaprabhu, a great devotee of Lord Hari, used to dance with ecstasy while chanting the name of God. Shri Ramakrishna Paramhansa, a great devotee of Goddess Kaali, would attain Samadhi while doing kirtan. He would remain in this blissful state, in complete oblivion of the outside world, for days together. Sai Baba also used to sing and dance in divine joy like a Sufi saint, chanting the name of God in *Takiya* at Shirdi (mentioned in Shri Sai Satcharita).

(iii) *Smaran* or *Manana* means thinking of the name, form, the attributes, and leelas of God. It is said that in Kaliyug, the greatest sadhana is chanting the name of God (smaran). Goswami Tulsi Das has mentioned in Shri Ram Charit Manas "*Naama saprema japa ta anayasa bhagat do hi muda mangla basa,*" which means that chanting the name of Shri Hari in Kaliyug is the means to attain welfare.

(iv), (v) and (vi), refer to *Padasevan, Archan,* and *Namaskar,* are synonymous with worshipping God in whatever form the devotee beholds. In Gita, Shri Krishna has stated that those devotees who worship Him or remember Him with true and unflinching love and devotion are very dear to Him and He takes their entire responsibility on Himself.

(vii) *Dasya* means rendering service to God with shradha, after becoming aware of His universal attributes like omniscience, omnipotence, and omnipresence. Shri Hanuman, a great devotee of Shri Lord Rama, is the best example in this category.

(viii) *Sakhyam* means considering God as a friend or *sakha* (companion) and lodging Him in one's heart. The gopis of Vrindavan had won over the heart of Lord Krishna with this *sakhya bhava*.

(ix) *Atmanivedan* is the last step of *Navadha Bhakti*. This means complete surrender of oneself to the Almighty Lord. In other words, one should surrender his body, mind, speech, and everything that matters, to the Lord and in return, accept whatever has been bestowed by God.

*****

26

Baba Knows Your Mind

In Vishnu Sahasranaam it has been mentioned that God is all knowing, and is in knowledge of the innermost secrets of everything in the universe. Though God is not easily perceived by our mind and body, yet He is aware of all the mysteries of the universe. History is replete with innumerable instances of how the incarnations of God can penetrate into the innermost minds of their devotees and disciples, influence them, and lead them to the best possible path, for their evolution and self-realization.

In December 1885, the great saint Shri Ramakrishna Paramhansa suffered from throat cancer. Acting upon the advice of the doctor, some of his dear devotees shifted him from the din and bustle of Kolkata city to a remote town called Kashipur. The cottage in which Shri Ramakrishna Paramhansa was staying had a beautiful garden in front. In the beginning, Shri Ramakrishna Paramhansa showed a marked improvement, which was due to the serenity and unpolluted environment. However, as time progressed, the pain increased because of deterioration in his health. So he had to be administered only a liquid diet. His body became inactive and his physical movements slowed down. He was hardly able to walk. Moreover, he would throw up whatever little food he used to take. Sometimes, when he used to cough, blood would come out from his throat. His chief disciple, Naren (Vivekananda), was very concerned at the failing health of his Thakur. A thought came to his mind which disturbed his mental peace: "Has God really incarnated in this physical body, constituting flesh and blood? How come he is not able to get rid of his own ailment? Although being the greatest devotee of Maa Kaali, why is he not invoking the deity's blessings to cure him and thereby get rid of his pain and suffering?"

Ramakrishna was then sleeping, with his eyes closed, when these thoughts flashed upon Naren's mind. Naren was sitting close by, keeping a vigil on his Thakur's physical condition. All of a sudden, he found his Thakur staring at him. In a very affectionate voice, Thakur addressed Naren and asked, "Have your doubts still not gone from your mind?" Pointing towards his body, he said, "Shri Rama of *Treta Yug* and Shri Krishna of *Dwapara Yug*, together constitute Shri Ramakrishna in me." Naren was astonished to hear these words. Thakur continued, "Whenever I behold my deity (Maa Kaali), I am in supreme bliss. I forget all about my health. Under such circumstances, how can I pray to my beloved Mother to cure me, when I have already surrendered my body, mind, ego, etc., at her feet?" Naren and the other disciples present there were astounded to hear these words from a great soul like Thakur Shri Ramakrishna Paramhansa, who had been reduced to a pale, frail, and sickly physical body.

In those times, contemporary Saint and Sadguru Shri Sainath of Shirdi, in Kopergaon Taluk of Ahmednagar district in Maharashtra, used to live in a dilapidated and abandoned masjid called Dwarkamayi. Attracted by His simplicity and divinity, thousands of devotees used to visit Shirdi for His blessings. These devotees were not only coming to Baba for His guidance, but they also considered Him as their saviour. They looked upon Him as their true friend-in-need and fondly addressed Him as Baba. In return, Sai Baba, very affectionately, kept them under His care, guidance, and protection. In the initial days of His arrival at Shirdi, people thought Him to be a mad fakir because of His indifferent behaviour. By and by, the village folks came to realize the greatness of this mad fakir when they subsequently witnessed His leelas. They not only saw the divinity in Baba and His great Yogic powers, which healed the sickly and diseased people, but also could fathom the omnipotence of Baba. His benevolent and sympathetic attitude drew innumerable devotees, who thronged Dwarkamayi just to have Baba's darshan and be blessed by Him.

Damodar Sawalram Rasne was a devotee of Baba, who hailed from Ahmednagar. He was a successful businessman. Rasne had been able to become the father of four children only with Baba's grace. Therefore, he was forever indebted to Him. He sought Baba's guidance at every step in his life, be it business or in domestic matters. Once, a few days before Baba's mahasamadhi, Rasne had visited Shirdi. While massaging Baba's legs and feet, he looked at Baba's frail body and a thought came across his mind, "What would happen to all devotees of Baba when He would pass away?" The second question which came to his mind was, "Several devotees visit Shirdi with materialistic and spiritual desires. Do they all get benefit from Baba's grace?" Although he was perturbed by these thoughts, he did not dare to ask Baba. But nothing was hidden from the omniscient Baba. Baba could read Rasne's thought instantaneously. He replied to both the questions which were in Rasne's mind.

To the first question Baba answered, *"Damiya, do you think that I am confined in this physical body of three and a half cubits? I shall be with you whenever and wherever you think of Me."* This promise He has kept when He was in His mortal body and even after 1918, when He took mahasamadhi. In response to the second question Baba replied, *"Look at the mango tree in bloom. If all the flowers become fruit, what a splendid crop it would be. But do they? Most fall off either as flowers or as unripe fruits due to wind, etc. Very few remain and grow to become fruits. Only those who are eligible for My grace will benefit."*

Hearing Baba's answers to his disturbing thoughts, Rasne was deeply moved and tears of gratitude rolled down his cheeks. The devotees who were present and listening to Baba could realize the significance of His words, that is, one must qualify oneself to get Baba's grace and blessings. Rasne has also clearly mentioned how he has been constantly guided by Baba in different circumstances, even after Baba's mahasamadhi.

In another incident, Baba was sitting in His darbar at Dwarkamayi masjid, surrounded by His devotees, when suddenly He said, "*My Gajanan is gone.*" The devotees were unable to understand the meaning of what He said. Some devotees related it to an elephant which was roaming about in the markets of Shirdi. They immediately rushed to the market where they found the elephant alive and roaming freely. Two days later, news arrived from Shegaon village of Maharashtra that Sadguru Advoot Gajanan Maharaj had left his mortal coil. And this had happened exactly at the time when Baba spoke the words, "*My Gajanan is gone.*" This was beyond the comprehension of the rustic folks. No doubt, the greatness of Baba is unparalleled.

*****

27

Crossing the Insurmountable

The fragrance of a flower spreads in all direction, on its own. Even if a fragrant flower blooms in a remote area, many get attracted by its fragrance. Similarly, Sai Baba of Shirdi, who resided in a dilapidated and abandoned masjid of a nondescript village in a remote corner of Maharashtra, could attract thousands of visitors — the poor and the rich, the elite and the illiterate, the high caste and the low caste. In spite of the rush of devotees to Shirdi, Baba remained unaffected and His daily routine was carried out uninterrupted till His mahasamadhi. When He was residing in Shirdi, His daily routine comprised visiting a few houses in Shirdi village and begging for alms, enquiring the welfare of the people of Shirdi, patiently listening to their woes in His darbar, speaking comforting words to them with sympathy and, at times, feeding the congregation of visitors at Dwarkamayi by cooking in a big handi (pot). Whoever approached Him with love and devotion, Baba used to receive and treat him with equal love and affection as if he was His own kith and kin and used to convey, through His words and actions, that He was their friend, philosopher, and guide.

In 1909, a reputed solicitor from Mumbai, Shri Hari Sitaram Dixit, arrived at Baba's darbar in Shirdi. He was a man of high position and status, besides being a very successful lawyer. He had fought and won a legal case in favour of Lokmanya Bal Gangadhar Tilak against the

British Raj and, by doing so, had incurred the wrath and displeasure of the British government. However, he had earned the goodwill of the society as a true patriot and a sincere worker of the Congress party. He became a member of Maharashtra Vidhan Parishad in the year 1901. In 1907, he had gone on a visit to London, where he met with an accident which resulted in the lameness of his leg. Even after receiving medical attention, the lameness of his leg could not be cured. His dear friend, Nanasaheb Chandorkar, was then the Deputy Collector of Ahmednagar. He was an ardent devotee of Sai Baba. He recommended Dixit to pay a visit to Shirdi and take Baba's darshan. Nana was convinced that his friend could be cured by Baba's blessings. He had firm faith in Baba and His divine powers. There were several instances where the sick and the diseased had been cured miraculously by Baba's touch and kind glance, childless couples had been blessed with children, and the mentally sick had got rid of their illness with Baba's grace. Kakasaheb Dixit could not avoid the continuous persuasion of his friend, Nanasaheb Chandorkar. Succumbing to his friend's wishes, he finally paid a visit to Shirdi. On reaching Shirdi, he came to Dwarkamayi and went to Baba's darbar. His first darshan of Baba brought about a remarkable transformation in him. His mind got composed and his entire being was filled with divine bliss. He forgot about the lameness of his body and wanted Baba to cure the lameness of his mind. Gradually, he felt no interest in materialistic gains. He left his lucrative profession, family, house, wealth, etc., and surrendered himself wholeheartedly to Baba. The rest of his life has been dedicated to the humble service of Baba.

The same feeling of dispassion towards worldly benefits also had come to the mind of Swami Vivekananda (affectionately addressed as Naren by Thakur Paramhansa). Swami Vivekananda had approached Thakur in a distressed state of mind. He was in a state of abject poverty because of his father's untimely demise. Being the eldest son, the entire responsibility of his family was on his shoulders. Thakur listened to the woes of Naren and advised him to pray before the Mother Goddess (Kaali), with clear cut instructions to open out his heart to Mother Goddess and, in return, all his desires would be fulfilled by her. But a very strange thing happened to Naren. When he prayed fervently to Maa, invoking Her blessings, he could not ask for any material objects. Instead, he prayed to Maa, "O Mother! Give me knowledge, devotion, and detachment from worldly things." Naren, in the divine company of Thakurji, had forgotten all about himself, his family, his financial condition, and wished upon himself indifference to all worldly attachments. What he wanted for himself was pure devotion and knowledge.

Similarly, Kakasaheb Dixit, in the divine presence of Sadguru Sainath, had become overwhelmed with love and devotion. His dispassion for worldly objects took over him and he asked Baba to cure the lameness of his mind rather than the lameness of his limb. He gave up his job, left all his property to his family members, and stayed at Shirdi to render service to Baba. He also built a house in Shirdi known as Dixit wada for devotees to stay. In the first floor of the building, he kept a room for himself.

He led a life of austerity and remained free from all worldly attachments. Under the divine guidance of Sai Baba, the spiritual progress of Kakasaheb Dixit could take place smoothly and steadily. Kakasaheb used to spend most of his time reading religious scriptures and texts, meditation, and chanting of hymns. His family members at Mumbai were highly displeased with his behaviour. His friends and relatives were shocked at Dixit's decision to leave his flourishing career and lead a secluded life. Some of them thought that Sai Baba of Shirdi was a tantric (one who has black magic powers) and imagined Kaka to be under His spell and control and, therefore, in great trouble. The reality was that Kakasaheb Dixit was in a state of ineffable bliss. He was immensely happy to be under the care and guidance of

Sadguru Sainath, who was not only his mentor and guru, but also his Lord (God). When his family came to Shirdi to persuade Dixit to return to Mumbai, Baba, in a very calm and reassuring manner told them, *"You need not worry about Kaka. I take his entire responsibility . . . ultimately, I shall take him in a viman (giving sadgati)."* Kaka had full faith in his Lord (Sai Baba).

Once, when Kakasaheb was in Shirdi, he received a message that his brother, who lived in Nagpur, was critically ill. Kaka read out the wireless message to Baba and said, "I am of no use to him." Baba immediately replied, *"So what, I shall be of use to him."* True to Baba's words, a sadhu had visited Kakasaheb's brother exactly at the time when Baba had mentioned that He would be of help to him. Blessing Kakasaheb's brother, the sadhu had said, *"Do not worry. I have come to help you. Be assured that from now onwards you shall be completely all right."* Later, when Kakasaheb received the message about his brother's recovery and how a sadhu had come to his rescue, he realized that the sadhu was none other than Sai Baba Himself. His conviction regarding Baba's powers of omniscience, omnipresence, and omnipotence were deeply reinforced.

After Baba's mahasamadhi in the year 1918, Kakasaheb took upon himself greater responsibilities. He became the Secretary of Sai Sansthan and contributed largely to spreading the gospel and message of Sai Baba. The journal published by Sai Sansthan known as *Sai Leela* is exemplary as it depicts the true stories and experiences of the devotees of Baba. These real life experiences have attracted lakhs of people towards Sai Baba and have inspired them to follow the Sai path. Truly, the contribution of Kakasaheb Dixit in spreading Baba's name and fame in the whole country is unmatched.

This great soul had departed on the auspicious Ekadashi day in July, 1926. On the fateful day, Kakasaheb Dixit was travelling in a train from Ville Parle to Mumbai with Annasaheb Dabholkar (author of Shri Sai Satcharita). Inside the train, both were deeply engrossed in singing Baba's glory when, all of a sudden, Kakasaheb fell on Annasaheb's shoulders and breathed his last. What a blessed departure! With Baba's name on his lips, he departed from this world blissfully, without any pain or anguish. Baba had said earlier, "*I shall take away my Kaka in a viman.*" The significance of Baba's words refers to sadgati or moksha. And true to His words, Baba had given sadgati to His dear devotee, Kakasaheb. How fortunate Kakasaheb was to have been blessed by Baba!

*****

28

Sai Liberates

It has been aptly mentioned in *Guru Gita* that, in order to attain self-realization, it is essential to have guru's *kripa* (grace). Just as a mirror is required to look at one's reflection, similarly, the guru's grace is essential to realize one's self. Here, guru means a Sadguru. A Sadguru is one who is not only proficient in the Shastras and Upanishads, but also is their exponent. He not only guides his disciples to the path of self-realization, but also enables them to achieve it. He removes the veil of ignorance and kindles the light of knowledge and wisdom. He is the embodiment of *Param Brahma*.

Sadgurus descend on this earth to perform a definite mission. They manifest on this earth in physical bodies and work for the disciples' spiritual upliftment as well as enable them to achieve sadgati. Param Sadguru Shri Sainath of Shirdi has often been observed to have remarked, *"If it is necessary, I may have to be reborn again and again in order to ensure sadgati for my devotees."* In reality, a Sadguru, by his divine grace and endless efforts, is capable of getting rid of the sins of his devotees accumulated over several lives and it is he who helps his devotees in treading the path of spiritual progress. He removes the evil habits of his devotees and destroys their ego, greed, and lust. Some devotees of the great saint, Shri Ramakrishna Paramhansa, once asked him how to achieve moksha. He replied, "Illusions create ego in the minds of people. They are an obstacle in the path of liberation. This illusion is like a curtain of clouds. Because of the clouds, the sun gets covered and is not visible to us. When this cloud cover is removed, the sun becomes visible. If, by guru's grace, these illusions are driven away and the ego is destroyed, then the darshan of the Lord is definitely possible."

In the third chapter of Gita, it has been explained that because of ego, a person thinks that he is the doer and makes the mistake of identifying his body, mind, and senses with the soul. Because of this illusion, he is intoxicated with the worldly and sensory pleasures. The great Rishi, Sanat Kumar, who was an embodiment of knowledge, has rightly said in *Sanat Sujatiya*, a treatise, that this illusion knells the death bell.

Only the Sadguru, who is a personification of truth, consciousness, and bliss (*Sat-Chit-Anand*), can remove this illusion. The *jiva* (being) comes in the grip of maya (illusion) and assumes many roles and forgets its own *swarupa* (self), though he is nothing but a part of *Satchidananda* (that is, God). Shri Ramakrishna Paramhansa has very succinctly explained that only God, from whom this maya emanates, can remove this maya. And the Sadguru, who is a manifestation of God, can also do so. Hence, the best way to get liberation is to take resort to Sadguru's feet.

There was a sanyaasi named Vijayanand who hailed from Chennai and had resorted to Baba's feet for attaining moksha. Though he had taken sanyaas, he was not free from worldly attachments. Baba was well aware of his nature. During his stay in Shirdi, he received a message from Chennai about his mother's illness. He felt sad and wanted to return home after taking Baba's permission. The omniscient Baba knew the future of the sanyaasi and said to him, "*If you loved your mother so much, why did you take sanyaas? Attachment makes misuse of an ochre garb. So leave all attachments and surrender yourself at the feet of the Lord. The Lord God will help you in attaining bliss.*"

Since Baba could foresee his impending death, He further advised him, *"Begin from tomorrow the study of Bhagwat. Read it conscientiously for three weeks. Your illusions will vanish and you will get eternal peace."* Vijayanand obeyed Baba's orders diligently. He completed two readings, after which he felt very exhausted. A couple of days, later he breathed his last. Thus, the sanyaasi could attain sadgati only through Baba's grace.

A few days before Baba's mahasamadhi, some people had visited Shirdi with a sickly and diseased tiger. They were the keepers of the ailing animal and lived on the income earned by exhibiting it. They had tried to cure it with all kinds of remedies, but their attempts had been futile. So they had come to Shirdi as the last resort. They hoped that Baba's miraculous powers would cure the sick animal. When the animal climbed up the steps of Dwarkamayi, it bowed down its head on account of the awe of Baba. Both looked at each other with love and affection for some time. Then, the animal dashed its tail on the floor of Dwarkamayi and breathed its last. How meritorious was the animal to have met its death at the feet of Baba!

Param Sadguru Shri Sainath, in a very lucid language, has told His devotees and other visitors assembled in His darbar, *"The real ignorance accrues from identifying your body, mind, and senses with your soul. Removal of this ignorance is knowledge. Physical body is impermanent, but the soul is everlasting and un-decaying. Maya arises due to this feeling of 'mine', that is, 'my' son, 'my' wife, 'my' house, and so on. Those who resort to maya are bound to suffer from misery. Hence, the real liberation is possible for one who is liberated from this maya. The grace of Sadguru could enable one to get this liberation and also liberation from this vicious circle of life and death. So offer yourself at the feet of your guru and get yourself liberated."*

*****

29

Where the Tomb Speaks

Sai Baba took mahasamadhi on 15 October, 1918, on the auspicious occasion of Dassehra. Far away from Shirdi, Smt. Pradhan, an ardent devotee of Sai Baba, became aware about Baba's demise. On that fateful day, when she was having her afternoon siesta, she dreamt of Baba shedding His mortal coil. Startled, she woke up, filled with grief. She wailed inconsolably and informed all those who were present that Baba was no more. That night she again had a dream. Baba appeared in her dream and said, *"My daughter! Saints never die. Even after taking Samadhi, they are ever alive and vigilant."* Baba has given this assurance to many of His devotees in Shirdi. Baba has often said to His devotees, *"Even after shedding this mortal body, I shall remain ever active and vigorous. My Samadhi shall talk to and bless My devotees according to their needs."* Now, long after Baba's mahasamadhi, the truth of this statement has been realized by numerous devotees.

B. V. Narasimha Swami, in 1936, met some devotees who were in personal contact with Baba when He was in His mortal coil while staying at Shirdi. Their personal experiences with Baba have all been compiled and published in a book titled *Devotees' Experiences*, which is a treasure house of incredible incidents that have taken place during Baba's lifetime, as well as after Baba's Samadhi. These experiences show that Sadgurus are ever-living and a constant source of inspiration and spiritual guidance.

Rao Bahadur S. B. Dhumal has remarked, "There is no incident in my life in which Baba's presence has not been felt. I believe every word I speak and every act I do is performed under His divine guidance. Baba is ever alive and active." This statement was made by Rao Bahadur Dhumal in the year 1936 to B. V. Narasimha Swami, that is, after eighteen years of Baba's mahasamadhi. Dhumal, who always used to abide by Baba's instructions, followed the same routine even after Baba's mahasamadhi, although in a different style. Whenever he required Baba's guidance, he would write the question and the possible solutions on different chits of paper. He would keep all these chits in the Samadhi Mandir. Taking Baba's name, he would pick up one chit. And he would abide by the instruction mentioned in the chit as if it was Baba's order. These instructions have always guided him correctly.

Another dear devotee of Sai Baba was Imam Bhai Chhote Khan. He visited Shirdi for the first time in the year 1910. Fakir Karvesh Shah had recommended him to pay a visit to Shirdi and take Baba's darshan. Eventually, he became an ardent devotee of Baba. In the year 1936, he was in dire need of money for performing his son's marriage. When Baba was living in Shirdi, many devotees approached Him to get rid of their financial, physical, and mental problems. Baba would listen to their woes most attentively, with sympathy and, then, help them in sorting out their problems.

Eighteen years had passed since Baba's mahasamadhi. Imam Bhai Chhote Khan did not know how to sort out his problem. With a meagre income, it was difficult for him to manage even the household expenses. He had no savings or any supplementary source of income. So he thought of taking recourse to Baba's feet. He went to Dwarkamaya masjid, Baba's abode in Shirdi, and prayed fervently to Baba to come to his rescue. That night Baba appeared in his dream and said, "*If you go to Pune, you will be successful in your endeavour.*" Abiding by Baba's instructions, he left for Pune. At Pune, he chanced to meet an old acquaintance of his. This person, named Ladkar, was suffering from ulcers and was in great agony. He remembered the medicine prescribed by Baba for the treatment of ulcer. He gave the same medicine to him. After taking the medicine, Ladkar felt better. In the meanwhile, Ladkar happened to win a horse race and from the prize money, he gave a gift of ₹700 to Chhote Khan, out of gratitude. With this amount, Chhote Khan was able to perform the marriage of his son smoothly.

Acharya Bharadhwaj, an ardent devotee of Sai Baba, in his book *Sadguru Sai Baba* has given a vivid description of the experiences of several devotees and how Baba's Samadhi Mandir talks to them and blesses them according to their needs and requirements. An instance from his book can be cited here. Chitnis, who was initially not a devotee of Baba, was so inspired seeing His portrait that he resolved to visit Shirdi and take Baba's darshan at the first opportunity. In the year 1952, he visited Shirdi for the first time and was very satisfied after taking darshan of Baba's portrait and Samadhi in the Samadhi Mandir. He felt as if he had come to a very beloved and familiar place. Later, he continued to visit Shirdi whenever he had an opportunity. In 1965, he suffered from acute pain in his stomach. The pain was so severe and intense that he was unable to drink even water. After a medical examination, he was advised by the doctor to go for an operation the following Thursday. In the meantime, Chitnis, who was very scared of surgery, prayed fervently to Baba to save him from the suffering. The same night he had a nightmare. He saw that four terrible looking persons were dragging and pushing him on his bed. However, at that moment, benevolent Sai came to his rescue and drove away the dreadful creatures. The next day, when he woke up, he had no pain and felt quite relieved. When he visited his doctor, to his great astonishment, he found that surgery was not required. Thus, by the grace of the merciful Lord Sainath and to the great joy of Chitnis, his surgery was averted.

K. D. Mhatre happened to visit Shirdi several years after Baba's mahasamadhi. At that time, repair work of the

Samadhi Mandir was being carried out. This Samadhi Mandir had been constructed by Bapusaheb Buti, a wealthy and affluent businessman from Nagpur. Initially, Lord Krishna's idol was supposed to be placed in the sanctum sanctorum of the mandir, whose construction work had started with Baba's consent and blessings. However, by the time the construction work got over, Baba had taken mahasamadhi and His last words had been, *"Place me at the centre."* In accordance with Baba's wishes, His mortal remains were placed in the central area of the shrine and the shrine became the Samadhi Mandir.

Once, Mhatre's two-and-a-half year old daughter was playing in the first floor of the Samadhi Mandir. Suddenly, she lost her balance and fell from the first floor. The people gathered in the hall rushed to pick her up. To their great surprise, she got up herself, before anybody could come to her rescue. With a radiant smile on her face, she said candidly, "That Old Man in the portrait (Baba's portrait placed in the Samadhi Mandir) caught me in His arms when I fell and very carefully He brought me down." At the time of this incident, Baba's idol had not yet been installed and prayers were being offered to Baba's portrait kept inside the Samadhi Mandir.

All these wonderful experiences illustrate the fact that although Baba has taken mahasamadhi in 1918, His devotees, even today, can connect with Him either by visiting the Samadhi Mandir to pay their obeisance to Him or simply by remembering Him. This is because Baba always fulfils the sincere wishes of His beloved devotees. A few days before taking mahasamadhi, Baba had assured His dear devotee, Damodar Sawalram Rasne, with the following words, *"Damiya* (sweet endearment of Baba)*! Why are you sad and worried about my departure from this world? Do you think I am confined in this physical body of three and a half cubits? Even after I shed this mortal body, I shall be with you whenever and wherever you think of Me."* This assurance of Baba is true in every word as has been experienced by one and all devotees.

*****

30

Rinanubandh

There is a saying that, at times, the disciples do not have to go in search of a guru. The guru himself beckons his shishyas. Sai Baba of Shirdi has often stated, "*I draw my men towards Me just like a bird is pulled by a string which is tied to its feet. I do not let My devotees to go farther away from My sight. I am accountable to God for the welfare of My devotees.*" The term *rinanubandh* implies a relationship of several generations, as well as a give-and-take relationship, due to past ties. In the context of the relationship that existed between Baba and His devotees, the relationship can be characterized as everlasting and permanent. Baba has remarked, "*I am a slave of My devotees. Their grief and pain are Mine. Till My devotees attain sadgati, I may have to take birth several times, if required.*"

Nanasaheb Chandorkar was a highly placed revenue official in Ahmednagar district. It was at this time that Baba had summoned Nana through Kulkarni, a junior revenue official. Nana was camping at Kopergaon Taluk when he received the invitation from Baba. Appa Kulkarni, at the behest of Baba, invited Nanasaheb to visit Shirdi. Nana was surprised at Baba's invitation and wondered how an ordinary fakir could have the audacity to send an invitation to a highly placed Government official like him. He flatly refused to come to Shirdi. However, Baba, without getting perturbed, sent an invitation to Nanasaheb through Kulkarni for the second time. This invitation was also unsuccessful. Then Baba sent a third invitation to Nanasaheb. Nanasaheb was perplexed at Baba's repeated invitations. Curiosity overtook him and he decided to pay a visit to Shirdi. After a few days, Nanasaheb left for Shirdi. On reaching Shirdi, he arrived at Dwarkamayi masjid and met Baba. He asked Baba what the reason was for inviting him to Shirdi. Baba's reply to him was very simple and straight forward. He said, *"We are related for four generations. You might have forgotten, but I have not. I want to revive our old connections."* The past, present, and future were known to the omniscient Sai Baba. He was aware of the fact that Nanasaheb was related closely to Him for the last four generations. So He was keen to renew the relationship and guide Nanasaheb to the path of self-realization.

The merciful Sai Baba has protected and come to the rescue of all His devotees whenever and wherever He has been invoked by their sincere prayers. There are several instances when Baba has saved Nanasaheb from calamities and troubles. Once, Nana and Lele Shastri were travelling in a tonga at Pune when, suddenly, the horse stumbled and the tonga turned upside down. This was a terrible accident and the consequences could have been fatal. However, the omniscient Sai Baba, with His ever protecting sight, could foresee the grave danger and averted it in time. When this accident took place at Pune, Baba was sitting in Dwarkamayi masjid, surrounded by His dear devotees. Suddenly, Baba made a gesture as if He was blowing a conch. The sound of the conch could be heard clearly and distinctly by all who were present in the masjid. In reality, there was no conch in Baba's hand! The blowing of conch symbolized the impending death of someone. At this moment, Baba had remarked, *"Nana is in the jaws of death. But I will not allow him to die so soon."* Nana and Lele Shastri were miraculously saved by Baba's grace and suffered no serious injury. Later, when they visited Shirdi, they came to know all that had happened at Shirdi at the time of their accident in faraway Pune. They were overwhelmed with gratitude towards Baba, their Saviour.

Nanasaheb realized the significance of Baba's statement to His devotees, *"If My devotee is in trouble, I will extend both My hands to save him. If required, I may extend all my limbs but I must save him from trouble."*

Once, Nanasaheb Chandorkar wanted to take darshan of the deity in a shrine located in the jungles of Padmalaya and also to pay his obeisance to the priest, Govind Bua, a holy person, who had his hermitage inside the temple premises. The temple was located twelve kilometres away from the railway station and in order to reach the temple, one had to travel about eight to nine kilometres through the jungle. Since the train had been late, Nana reached the railway station late in the night. By that time his office staff, who had come to receive him, had gone back. It was quite dark. However, Nana was determined to visit the temple. So, along with his companions, he walked the entire stretch of the path through the jungle. The journey was quite arduous and Nana was very hungry. Usually, the priest of the temple, after the evening aarti, would lock the main door of the sanctum sanctorum and leave for his home, which was at a little distance from the temple. Since it was quite late, Nana expected that the priest would have left for his home. He remembered Baba and prayed to Him, "Oh Baba! At the end of the journey, how nice it would be to get a hot cup of tea to quench my thirst as well as to overcome the tiredness. How wonderful it would be to meet Govind Bua!"

By the time they reached the temple, it was past ten in the night. But to the amazement of Nana and his friends, the door of the temple was open and they were welcomed and received by none other than the priest of the temple, Govind Bua. On seeing them, he asked, "Has Nanasaheb come?" Wonderstruck to hear his name Nana addressed the priest very politely, "How did you know that I was coming to visit the shrine?" Govind Bua's reply was still more wonderful. He said, "I received an ethereal message from Sai Baba. In His message, Baba said, *'My Nana will reach there after some time. You should wait for him and offer Nana and his friends hot cups of tea.'* That's why I have prepared tea for you and was waiting for your arrival." Nana gratefully remembered the ever-caring Baba's benediction. The good deeds and merits of Nanasaheb Chandorkar over the last several lives, as well as his complete surrender to his Guru, Sai Baba, subsequently, had drawn him to Sai Baba due to rinanubandh.

*****

31

All Pilgrimages Lead to Shirdi

It is a strong belief among the Hindus that Prayag, the confluence of the holy rivers of Ganga, Yamuna, and the mythical Saraswati, is the most important destination for all pilgrims. Hindus believe that a holy dip at Prayag is very auspicious and washes away all the sins of human beings. Prayag is located at Allahabad, in Uttar Pradesh. During Kumbh and Ardha Kumbh (Kumbh occurs once in twelve years and Ardha Kumbh occurs once in six years), people in large numbers from all parts of the country assemble at Prayag to take a holy bath.

Once, a very dear devotee of Sai Baba, Dasganu Maharaj, was keen to visit Prayag to take a holy bath. With this desire in mind, he came to Shirdi to take Baba's permission. Baba's reply in response to Dasganu's request surprised all those who were present, including Dasganu himself. Baba had replied in a very serious tone, *"You need not go so far. Our Prayag is here only. Believe Me."* Dasganu was bewildered and did not know what to say after hearing Baba's strange reply. However, he had firm faith in his Sadguru and he bowed down at Baba's feet in prostration. He was stunned to see that two streams of water were trickling down from Baba's toes. What an amazing sight! He was simply wonderstruck. Were Baba's words true? Were the two streams of water from Ganga and Yamuna? Was it true that Prayag was located here itself, at the very feet of Baba? His throat was choked with emotions and his eyes were filled with tears of joy. Collecting a handful of water from Baba's toes, he sprinkled it upon himself as well as upon others who were present there. He felt blessed and composed a vandana (hymn), that is, a song in praise of Lord Sainath) in Marathi, while enjoying this blissful moment.

Shirdi majhe Pandarpura, Sai Baba Ramavara;
Shuddha bhakti Chandrabhaga, Bhava Pundalik Jaga.

The verse means that Shirdi is our Pandharpur (Pandharpur is a place of pilgrimage which has been dedicated to the worship of Vithal deity, that is, Lord Vishnu, in the main shrine). At Shirdi, our Lord Sai Baba resides, who is the incarnation of Lord Vishnu. Beholding Baba, our flow of bhakti surges, just like the waves of the river Chandrabhaga. And all pure feelings of love and devotion arise for our Sainath, who epitomises Lord Vithal of Pandharpur.

All doubts vanished from Dasganu's mind. He was convinced that Shirdi was his Prayag—the holy confluence. So there was no need to undertake a trip to the faraway Prayag. Just like a dip in the holy confluence gets rid of all our sins and demerits, similarly, surrendering at the holy feet of our guru also enables us to get rid of our sins, our vices, and ego. Because our guru, who is our preceptor and spiritual guide, helps us not only to tread on the path of righteousness, but also enables us to achieve self-realization. Therefore, all kinds of meditation, prayers, and pilgrimages culminate at the holy feet of our Sadguru. Dasganu realized that grace of Sainath (his Guru and God), would help him to cross the mundane world because the Almighty had manifested on this earth in the form of Sainath. He spent the rest of his life in the service of Baba and was responsible for spreading Baba's name and fame in every nook and corner of Maharashtra through his soul-stirring kirtans and melodious bhajans.

In this context, the true life story of Durga Charan Nag may be mentioned. He happened to be a staunch devotee of

Thakurji, Shri Ramakrishna Paramhansa. Although a family man, he wanted to renounce his family and lead the life of a sanyaasi in the ashram and for this purpose he approached Thakurji to seek permission for the same. But Thakurji's response to his request was different. He said, "What is the problem in leading the life of a householder? A householder leads a protected life in the confines of the house, unaffected from the vagaries of the world. Engage yourself in bhagwad chintan (meditating on God)."

Thakurji's counselling impacted Nag and he gave up his desire to renounce his family, nor did he ever neglect his duties towards them. However, leaving behind his medical profession (he was a homeopath); he lived a simple and pious life in his native village and became an exemplary practioner for the sanyaasis and sadhus of the Ramakrishna Order.

Once, on the auspicious occasion of Ardhadoya Yoga (this occurs once in fifty years), Durga Charan Nag decided to travel from Kolkata to his native village, Deobhog (now located in Bangladesh). His father, Dindayal, did not approve of his decision. During Ardhadoya Yoga lakhs of devotees assemble at the Ganga Sagar ghat near Kolkata to take a holy bath in the Ganges. It is believed that a dip in the holy Ganga on that day would get rid of all the sins of present as well as past lives. So his father strongly objected to the idea of leaving Kolkata and travelling, instead of taking a holy bath during this auspicious time. However, the calm and composed Durga Charan Nag very candidly confessed, "If a person has real faith, then Mother Ganges will bless the person by appearing in his house. There is no need to travel elsewhere."

Durga Charan Nag had many visitors, guests, and young sadhus from the Ramakrishna Mission in his house during the occasion of Ardhadoya Yoga. One day, a young sanyaasi observed a thin stream of water emerging from below the ground in the south-east corner of the courtyard. Others who were present on the occasion keenly watched the scene when, gradually, the thin stream became a smooth flow of water. Nag arrived at the spot and, with reverence to Mother Ganga (Ganga is considered as a Mother Goddess and worshipped by the Hindus). He collected some water which was flowing and sprinkled it upon himself. Overwhelmed with devotion, he offered his prayers to Maa Ganga, "O Mother Ganga! Victory be to you. Make us pure by showering your blessings."

The news of this incredible incident spread to nearby villages. Thousands flocked to Nag's house to pay their obeisance to Mother Ganga, as well as to take the holy bath. They all felt fortunate to have been blessed by Mother Ganga and rejoiced to have got this wonderful opportunity. Several days later, Swami Vivekananda, a very eminent disciple of Shri Ramakrishna Paramhansa, remarked on this incident, "A great soul like Durga Charan Nag can make possible through his wishes what is actually impossible. His strong willpower can give moksha to any human being."

*****

32

Surrendering to Guru

Surrendering to one's own guru is of great significance in the path of *Gurumarg*. In this context, Sai Baba has spoken very clearly, "*Surrender your body, mind, and speech at the lotus feet of your guru. In other words, you must surrender yourself completely to your guru. And then watch, what he does for you.*"

Nanasaheb Chandorkar, an ardent devotee of Baba, was well-versed in the Shastras, Vedas, and Vedantas. Once, while reciting a shloka from the Bhagwad Gita, spoke the following sentence: *Tadvidhi Pranipatena Pariprashnena Sevaya.* Baba, who was listening to Nana, asked him to explain the meaning of the words *Pranipata, Pariprashna,* and *Seva.* Nana tried to explain the meaning and significance implied by each word. However, Baba was not convinced with Nana's elucidation of the terms. Therefore, He explained as follows: "*Mere prostration before the guru in the form of sastang pranam is not enough. The actual implication of Pranipata is `atmanivedan'. The disciple cannot receive the grace of his guru unless and until he has completely surrendered himself to his guru in the true sense. When he surrenders his ego and identity completely and takes resort to his guru's feet, then he becomes aptly qualified to receive the wealth of knowledge from his guru.*"

In the context of *Pariprashna,* Baba has stated that it is essential that the curiosity and inquisitiveness of a disciple must be satiated. However, the queries pertaining in the context must be valid and not asked either to harass the guru or asked just for the sake of asking. Just to show off one's knowledge or to test the wisdom of one's guru or asking questions with evil intentions does not befit an intelligent disciple.

With regard to s*eva*, Baba has said, *"When inclined I shall serve, otherwise not – this feeling does not imply seva in true sense. A person should realize that he himself is not the master of his physical body and that his body belongs to his guru and the very purpose of his body is to serve his guru only."* In this context, Baba has cited the instance of His own guru. Baba has described His guru in the following words, *"My guru, in fact, was an epitome of love and affection. I am indebted to My guru for permitting Me to stay with him and serve him. Forgetting hunger and thirst, I used to gaze at My guru with unblinking eyes. He was the focal point of my concentration and meditation. He was my only source of refuge. In return, My guru had asked Me two paisa as `dakshina'. I had gladly given those two paisa as guru dakshina. The two paisa he had asked for were shradha and saburi. By demonstrating unflinching faith or shradha towards My guru, as well as by serving my guru with patience and perseverance for years together, I had dedicated those two paise to my guru."*

Swami Vivekananda, a favourite disciple of Shri Ramakrishna Paramhansa and a great authority over the Vedas and Vedantas, has also stated in one of his deliberations, *"Oh citizens of Bharat (India)! Do not forget that you owe your body to your mother since the time you were born. If during your lifetime, name, fame, and wealth are bestowed upon you by divine blessings, then what should we surrender to God? This question may arise in the minds of many, which is a natural phenomenon. Only those virtues can be surrendered to God which are owned by us. In the event of such a case, we should surrender our ego, which is the actual form of self-surrender. When the ego is annihilated, the self becomes one entity with God."* Sai Baba of Shirdi has also spoken in this context, *"One who gets rid of his ego and meditates on God with complete devotion and faith will be liberated from the shackles of attachment and shall attain moksha."*

Navadha Bhakti also illustrates the virtues of self-surrender and self-renunciation. In the eighteenth chapter of Gita (*Moksha, Sanyaas, Yoga*) Shri Krishna has given firm assurance to Arjun with the following words, "*Let Me be the abode of your conscience. Surrender yourself completely to Me with devotion and faith and, in return, you shall attain Me.*" This statement implies that the Lord God should be made the prime object of concentration, as well as regarded as the sole source of refuge in order to attain *parmartha* (goal of life). Similarly, Param Sadguru Shri Sainath, the God-incarnation of the Kaliyug, has also said in this context, "*One who surrenders himself completely to Me and remembers Me always, I am indebted towards him. I repay this debt by giving him moksha in the form of self-realization.*" Baba has often been observed to have remarked, "*One who has accepted this fakir as his sole refuge, this fakir shall never disappoint him.*" These were not mere words but absolute truth, as has been experienced by innumerable devotees who have completely surrendered to Sai Baba and accepted Him as their Lord God.

Once, a devotee of Baba who lived far away from Shirdi wanted to visit Dwarkamayi, along with his family. But just before embarking on his journey, he fell ill. Suffering from high fever, he was unable to go to Shirdi. However, he persuaded his family to make the trip and gave some money to his son, which was to be offered to Baba as dakshina. The family reached Shirdi and went to Dwarkamayi for Baba's darshan. Abiding by his father's wishes, the son offered the dakshina to Baba. As soon as Baba accepted the dakshina, He started shivering and had high fever. Observing the shivering in Baba's body, the devotees assembled in the darbar enquired from Baba the reason. Baba smilingly gave them the reply, "*I have accepted the dakshina of My devotee. Is it not my duty to show concern about his welfare?*" By doing so, Baba had taken upon himself the sufferings of that devotee and from the moment Baba accepted his dakshina, the devotee completely recouped from fever.

In another instance, R. B. Purandar had planned a visit to Shirdi, along with his wife, for taking Baba's darshan. Coming to know about their intended visit to Shirdi, Smt. Tarkhad, out of great devotion, gave them two brinjals for Baba. She requested Smt. Purandar to prepare *bharit* of one brinjal and *bhajiya* of the other one and offer it to Baba as naivedya on her behalf. After reaching Shirdi, Smt. Purandar prepared *bharit* of one brinjal and offered it to Baba. There were several delicacies which had already been offered to Baba as naivedya. However, Baba chose to have the offering of *bharit* from Smt. Purandar. With great relish, He ate the *bharit* and commented, *"How tasty this bharit is! Now get the bhajiya. That will add more to the taste!"* The devotees who were present in the masjid were in a difficulty. Since it was not the season of brinjals, they wondered how to procure a brinjal for bhajiya. When they asked who had brought the bharit, they found that Smt. Purandar had also been entrusted with the responsibility of serving bhajiya to Baba. Everybody then realized the significance of Baba's desire to eat bhajiya. They were, indeed, wonderstruck at Baba's all pervasive knowledge. Here Baba wanted to illustrate that any offering served with love and devotion is accepted gladly by God. In this context, Baba has remarked, *"Whoever thinks of only Me, is desperate to get Me, and eats nothing without first offering it to Me, he is my true devotee. Anybody who approaches Me with this bhav (feeling), he becomes one with Me, just like a river merges into the sea."*

*****

33

Trikaldarshi Baba

V ishnu Sahasranaam describes Baba with the following characteristic features:

> *Sarvadarshi Vimuktatma*
> *Sarvangya Gyanamuttammam*

God is *Sarvadarshi* means that God is omniscient, that is, He has knowledge of all the actions performed by all living beings. God is *Vimuktatma* (detached), which means He is free from all attachments. God is *Sarvangya* (all knowledgeable), because He commands holistic knowledge of the entire universe and, lastly, God is *Gyanamuttammam*, that is, He is the epitome of Supreme knowledge and is not limited to any dimension be it time, object, or place. Sadgurus, who are, in reality, the incarnations of God, descend on earth to fulfil the specific mission of God, that is, enabling all their disciples to realize God or Self. This is possible because they possess all the essential qualities of God — all-knowing, all-pervasive, and all-powerful.

Nanasaheb Chandorkar was a dear devotee of Param Sadguru Sainath of Shirdi. He was a high ranking officer in the Revenue Department. He was also well-versed in all Hindu scriptures. He used to visit Shirdi often to pay his obeisance to Baba. He visited the Dattatreya Shrine at Kopergaon regularly, on his way to Shirdi. Once, the priest at Dattatreya Shrine requested Nanasaheb for some money, which was needed for the maintenance of the temple. Nanasaheb agreed and promised to donate three hundred rupees toward the repair work of the temple, on his subsequent visit. Soon after, he got an opportunity to visit Shirdi again. However, in the meantime, he had not been able to arrange the necessary funds, which he had committed to donate to the priest at the Dattatreya Shrine. So, instead of taking the usual route and paying obeisance to Lord Dattatreya, he thought of taking a detour to Shirdi. Reluctantly, he took the detour, which was a difficult route, with lots of thorny bushes on the way. He was hurt when a sharp thorn struck him on his feet. With great difficulty, he reached Shirdi and went to Dwarkamayi to take Baba's darshan. Strangely, Baba showed no enthusiasm to receive Nanasaheb. Nanasaheb was taken aback at Baba's indifferent behaviour. Baba sat quietly, with a disapproving look, for a long time, to the dismay of Nanasaheb. Completely fatigued after the arduous journey, Nanasaheb addressed Baba, "Baba, are you annoyed with me? Why are you so quiet? Will you not talk to me?" Baba replied, "*Yes, I don't want to talk to you. Just because you could not arrange the requisite funds for the Dattatreya temple, did you have to take a longer and winding path to Shirdi? For this trifle reason, you avoided the darshan of Dattatreya Shrine. No harm would have been caused if you would have simply expressed to the priest your inability to arrange the necessary funds. After remaining in my company for so long, such kind of behaviour is simply not expected*".

Hearing Baba's reason for displeasure, Nanasaheb was filled with remorse. Nana realized that Baba was keeping track of all his movements, even while sitting at Dwarkamayi. Since nothing could be hidden from the omniscient Sai Baba, he took a firm resolution to act in accordance with propriety and follow the divine path shown by Baba. Baba is *Trikaldarshi*, that is, He knows the past, present, and the future.

In another incident, another close devotee of Baba, Shri Damodar Sawalram Rasne, who Baba fondly addressed as

Damiya, wanted Baba's advice for his business. At that time, investment in cotton speculation seemed to be attractive and profitable. Before taking the plunge, he wanted Baba's approval. So he wrote a letter to Shama, a dear devotee of Baba, to seek permission from Him on his behalf. Shama had still not read out the contents of the letter when Baba spoke, *"What does this Damiya want? He wants to earn in lakhs. Ask him to be contented with what Allah has given him. He should not crave for more."* Damiya was disappointed with Baba's reply. So he came to Shirdi and paid his obeisance to Baba. While massaging Baba's feet, he had a fleeting thought that if Baba permitted him to invest in cotton speculation, he would gladly donate a portion of his profits as dakshina to Baba. When Damiya was thinking in this manner, Baba spoke suddenly, *"What do I have to do with your profits? I am a fakir. What does a fakir require? A small amount of alms will suffice my needs. However, I had advised you for your good."* That antaryami Baba could read his thoughts and reprimand him, came as a surprise to Damiya. After Baba's advice, he dare not invest in cotton speculation. That year, cotton speculation proved to be a loss making venture. Damiya was fortunate enough to be saved from a terrible loss because of Baba's grace and timely intervention.

Swami Paramhansa Yogananda in his book *Autobiography of a Yogi* has given a vivid description of a subtle experience during his stay in the ashram at Srirampur. One afternoon his guru, Swami Yukteswar Giri, was explaining the essence of the Shastras to his disciples. Swami Yogananda was sitting with the disciples when his guru spoke suddenly, "Mukund (Swami Yogananda's first name), you are not listening carefully to what I am saying." Mukund replied, "I have heard all what you have said. I can explain everything that you have just said." But Swami Yukteswar Giri replied, "Is it not true that you are thinking in your mind about three buildings—one located in the plains, the second located at the seashore, and the third located in the hills?" Mukund was embarrassed and filled with guilt for his unbecoming behaviour. He was awestruck as to how his guru, with his sharp, ever vigilant eyes, could penetrate into the innermost part of his mind and know his thoughts. This was a great revelation of the guru's supernatural powers!

His omniscient guru said, "It is true that, in due course of time, these three institutions will develop exactly at those places as you have perceived. But, right now, you should understand the meaning and underlying knowledge of the Shastras. Even though I do not want to enter into your innermost thoughts, I am doing so as a part of my duty to regulate your thought process. Since you have surrendered your present as well as your future to me, I, as your guru, must ensure that you are focused in your present and enable you to realize the self."

Sadgurus, who can see the present and future because of their divine powers, use their omniscience to protect their disciples and devotees from all evils and guide them in the righteous path.

*****

34

Sairupadhar Raghavottam

In the Indian culture and Hindu mythology, the incarnation Shri Rama has been presented as *Maryada Purush* — the symbol of purity, sacrifice, and righteousness. For all these virtues, Shri Rama has been assigned the titles of *Raghu Kula Bhushan* (the jewel of Raghu dynasty) or *Raghavottam*. Similarly, towards the last part of the nineteenth century and in the first two decades of the twentieth century, a small nondescript village called Shirdi, in the state of Maharashtra, found a divine being in the form of Shri Sainath. Sainath, who had made this remote village His abode, was an epitome of benevolence, sacrifice, love, dedication, and service to mankind. Baba's selfless service towards His disciples and devotees, as well as His motherly care and affection remains, till today, incomparable. His divinity and supernatural powers liken Him to God. And His devotees fondly address Him as *Sai Ram* because of similar attributes.

In the *Sai Mahima* shloka of Sai Aarti, Sai Baba has been presented as:

Sai Rupadhar Raghavottam
Bhaktakam Vividhadrumam Prabhum

This means that Sai is a *roop* (form) of Shri Rama, who fulfils all the desires of His devotees. The essence of the character of Shri Rama was to honour one's word irrespective of the consequences, perform one's duty to the society even at great personal cost, give protection to those who have surrendered, accept the love and devotion of the subjects and reciprocate with equal love and affection, destroy the evil forces and protect the weak and vulnerable, as well as show perfect regard and respect towards saints and seers. These were the special qualities associated with the Shri Rama avatar. In a similar manner, Sai Baba, a benefactor of His devotees, would share the pains and sorrow of every devotee and visitor who surrendered to Him. He would listen to their tales of woes, misery, and misfortunes with complete attention, concern, and patience. Those who would take shelter at the lotus feet of Baba, received Baba's mercy and grace. Baba would not only get rid of their pain and afflictions but, in many cases as has been revealed in Shri Sai Satcharita, He would take upon Himself their diseases and troubles. He would take care of their material as well as spiritual aspirations. This is why His devotees have adorned Him with the title of *Samarth Sadguru Sainath Maharaj*.

Sai Baba spent most of His life in Shirdi. In the initial days of His stay in Shirdi, Baba would take care of the village folks by personally visiting their houses. If anybody was sick, Baba used to cure him with His *jadi-buti*. Later on, He stopped this practice and would bless anyone who came to Him by distributing udi. Udi was collected from the sacred dhuni which was kept perpetually burning in Dwarkamayi masjid by Baba. The speciality of udi was that Baba regarded it as *mahausadhi* (prime medicine and the chief cure for all maladies). Baba used to apply udi in the areas of the body which was afflicted and also gave udi as prasad for curing the physical and mental ailments of his devotees.

The doors of Dwarkamayi masjid were open to all, irrespective of religion, caste, and creed as well as the rich and the poor, the literate and the illiterate, the atheists and the non-atheists. As time progressed, the flow of visitors, disciples, and devotees to Shirdi increased significantly. These visitors came to Shirdi to seek Baba's blessings, to be cured of their physical and mental afflictions, and also for their spiritual progress. Many would be wonderstruck at the divine powers of Baba. Although Baba was a poor fakir who survived by begging alms from the village folks and had made a dilapidated masjid His resting place, He could attract lakhs of visitors to Shirdi and motivate them to follow the spiritual path. Indeed, all visitors were convinced that whoever puts his feet on the soil of Shirdi, would become free from troubles, woes, anguish, and misery by the grace of Lord Sainath. Baba, an embodiment of compassion, is fondly addressed by His followers and devotees as *Sai Mauli* (Sai Mother) in Marathi.

A close devotee of Baba, Shama, once asked Him, "Oh Deva! Why are you wasting your time and energy for these people who come to you only with selfish desires and materialistic aspirations? If you permit, I will stop them from bothering you unnecessarily." Merciful Sainath immediately replied, "*Oh Shama! Do not refuse them. I am sitting in this masjid only to listen to their woes. In reality, I have summoned them from far flung places. After fulfilling their mundane desires, I shall lead them in the spiritual path.*"

Baba would remain so engrossed in the worldly problems of the devotees that He would forget about His own food and would hardly find any time even to take rest. The entire night, Baba would remain wide awake, vigilant, and meditate to the Almighty Lord for the welfare of His devotees. In the process, He would neglect His own health. Slowly, His health started deteriorating and Baba became lean and feeble. Once, a dear devotee of Baba, Dadasaheb Khaparde, felt very worried and concerned about Baba's failing health and started weeping. Baba consoled Khaparde in a reassuring tone and said, "*What I can see is My health shall remain in such a condition till I depart. However, there is nothing to worry in this regard. I shall take care of My devotees as long as I am in this mortal body and will continue to take care of all their problems even when I leave this physical body.*"

There are several instances when Baba has taken upon Himself the pain and sufferings of His devotees. Once, Dadasaheb Khaparde was staying in Shirdi with his family when his young son contracted Bubonic plague. Smt. Khaparde panicked because, in those days, Shirdi lacked medical facilities. With tears in her eyes, she ran to her saviour, Sai Baba, and sought His permission to leave for Amravati for medical assistance. Baba, seeing her plight, calmed her down and reassured her, "*You have nothing to fear or worry. I take away the pains and sufferings of My devotees because they are My children and their difficulties are Mine.*" Saying thus, Baba lifted His kafni to show four fully developed buboes on His body to all who were present. Miraculously, at that very moment, the buboes which had developed on Smt. Khaparde's son vanished without any trace. Smt. Khaparde was overwhelmed with gratitude to Baba for showering His mercy on her ailing son. This is a clear testimony to the fact that Baba took upon Himself the sufferings of His devotees. This is the special trait of Baba, an embodiment of love and mercy!

Today, after many decades of Baba's mahasamadhi, people visit Shirdi in large numbers to pay their respects to Sainath in the Dwarkamayi masjid and the Samadhi Mandir. Baba's statement in this context, "*My tomb shall speak, bless, and take care of all problems of My devotees according to their needs,*" has proved to be absolutely true. Devotees pay their obeisance to Sai Baba, exhibit unflinching faith and devotion towards Him, and participate in all the aartis at Shirdi with spiritual fervour.

There is no evidence about the exact date of birth of Sai Baba. His date of birth and early childhood remain a mystery to all of us. Baba, Himself, has never said anything in this context. During His stay at Shirdi, the auspicious festival of Ramnavami of the Hindus and the Urs festival of the Muslims were simultaneously and enthusiastically celebrated without any hitch. Later on, some years before Baba's mahasamadhi, people started celebrating Ramnavami as Baba's birth anniversary. His devotees used to address Him very fondly as Sai Ram because of the great similarities in the characteristics and features of both the incarnations. Both the incarnations embody love, compassion, righteousness, and a sense of caring and protection towards their devotees.

*****

Our Books on SHIRDI SAI BABA

Shirdi Sai Baba is a household name in India as well as in many parts of the World today. These books offer fascinating glimpses into the life and miracles of Shirdi Sai Baba and other Perfect Masters. These books will provide you with an experience that is bound to transform one's sense of perspective and bring about perceptible and meaningful spiritual growth.

The Eternal Sai Consciousness
A. R. Nanda
ISBN 978 81 207 9043 8
₹ 200

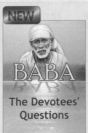

BABA:
The Devotees' Questions
Dr. C. B. Satpathy
ISBN 978 81 207 8966 1
₹ 150

The Loving God:
Story of Shirdi Sai Baba
Dr. G. R. Vijayakumar
ISBN 978 81 207 8079 8
₹ 200

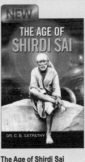

The Age of Shirdi Sai
Dr. C. B. Satpathy
ISBN 978 81 207 8700 1
₹ 225

Sai Samartha and Ramana Maharshi
S. Seshadri
ISBN 978 81 207 8986 9
₹150

Shri Sai Satcharita
The Life and Teachings of Shirdi Sai Baba
Translated by Indira Kher
ISBN 978 81 207 2211 8
₹ 500(HB)
ISBN 978 81 207 2153 1
₹ 300(PB)

Sree Sai Charitra Darshan
Mohan Jagannath Yadav
ISBN 978 81 207 8346 1
₹ 200

Baba's Divine Symphony
Vinny Chitluri
ISBN 978 81 207 8485 7
₹ 250

Sai Baba an Incarnation
Bela Sharma
ISBN 978 81 207 8833 6
₹ 200

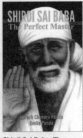

Shirdi Sai Baba: The Perfect Master
Suresh Chandra Panda & Smita Panda
ISBN 978 81 207 8113 9
₹ 200

SHIRDI within & beyond
A collection of unseen & rare photographs
Dr. Rabinder Nath Kakarya
ISBN 978 81 207 7806 1
₹ 750

Shri Sai Baba
Teachings & Philosophy
Lt Col M B Nimbalkar
ISBN 978 81 207 2364 1
₹ 100

The Eternal Sai Phenomenon
A R Nanda
ISBN 978 81 207 6086 8
₹ 200

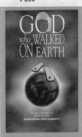

God Who Walked on Earth:
The Life & Times of Shirdi Sai Baba
Rangaswami Parthasarathy
ISBN 978 81 207 1809 8
₹ 150

STERLING

Baba's Rinanubandh
Leelas during His Sojourn in Shirdi
Compiled by Vinny Chitluri
ISBN 978 81 207 3403 6
₹ 200

Baba's Gurukul
SHIRDI
Vinny Chitluri
ISBN 978 81 207 4770 8
₹ 200

Baba's Anurag
Love for His Devotees
Compiled by Vinny Chitluri
ISBN 978 81 207 5447 8
₹ 125

Baba's Vaani: His Sayings and
Teachings
Compiled by Vinny Chitluri
ISBN 978 81 207 3859 1
₹ 200

The Gospel of Shri Shirdi Sai
Baba: A Holy Spiritual Path
Dr Durai Arulneyam
ISBN 978 81 207 3997 0
₹ 150

Jagat Guru: Shri Shirdi
Sai Baba
Prasada Jagannadha Rao
ISBN 978 81 207 8175 7
₹ 100

Spotlight on the Sai Story
Chakor Ajgaonker
ISBN 978 81 207 4399 1
₹ 125

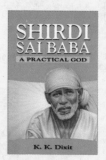

Shirdi Sai Baba
A Practical God
K. K. Dixit
ISBN 978 81 207 5918 3
₹ 75

Life History of Shirdi Sai Baba
Ammula Sambasiva Rao
ISBN 978 81 207 7722 4
₹ 150

I am always with you
Lorraine Walshe-Ryan
ISBN 978 81 207 3192 9
₹ 150

BABA- May I Answer
C.B. Satpathy
ISBN 978 81 207 4594 0
₹ 150

Unravelling the Enigma: Shirdi Sai
Baba in the light of Sufism
Marianne Warren
ISBN 978 81 207 2147 0
₹ 400

STERLING

**Shirdi Sai Baba
The Divine Healer**
Raj Chopra
ISBN 978 81 207 4766 1
₹ 100

**Shirdi Sai Baba and
other Perfect Masters**
C B Satpathy
ISBN 978 81 207 2384 9
₹ 150

The Miracles of Sai Baba
ISBN 978 81 207 5433 1 (HB)
₹ 250

Sai Hari Katha
Dasganu Maharaj Translated by
Dr. Rabinder Nath Kakarya
ISBN 978 81 207 3324 4
₹ 100

Shri Sai Baba- The Saviour
Dr. Rabinder Nath Kakarya
ISBN 978 81 207 4701 2
₹ 100

Sai Baba's 261 Leelas
Balkrishna Panday
ISBN 978 81 207 2727 4
₹ 125

Sri Sai Baba
Sai Sharan Anand
Translated by V.B Kher
ISBN 978 81 207 1950 7
₹ 200

Sai Baba: His Divine Glimpses
V B Kher
ISBN 978 81 207 2291 0
₹ 95

**Ek An English Musical on the
Life of Shirdi Sai Baba**
Usha Akella
ISBN 978 81 207 6842 0
₹ 75

**A Diamond Necklace To:
Shirdi Sai Baba**
Giridhar Ari
ISBN 978 81 207 5868 1
₹ 200

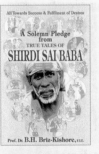

**A Solemn Pledge from
True Tales of
Shirdi Sai Baba**
Dr B H Briz-Kishore
ISBN 978 81 207 2240 8
₹ 95

**Shri Shirdi Sai Baba: His
Life and Miracles**
ISBN 978 81 207 2877 6
₹ 30

STERLING

SHIRDI SAI BABA

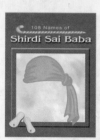

**108 Names of
Shirdi Sai Baba**
ISBN 978 81 207 3074 8
₹ 50

Shirdi Sai Baba Aratis
ISBN 978 81 207 8456 7
(English)　₹ 10

**Shirdi Sai Speaks...
Sab Ka Malik Ek**
Quotes for the Day
ISBN 978 81 207 3101 1
₹ 200

**The Thousand Names of
Shirdi Sai Baba**
Sri B.V. Narasimha Swami Ji
Hindi translation by
Dr. Rabinder Nath Kakarya
ISBN 978 81 207 3738 9
₹ 75

Shirdi Sai Baba Box

Shri Sai Baba
978 81 207 6920 5
Box size: 23.5 x 16.5 cm
₹ 900

Shri Sai Satcharitra

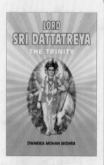

**Lord Sri Dattatreya
The Trinity**
Dwarika Mohan Mishra
ISBN 978 81 207 5417 1
₹ 200

Vibhuti

Sai Baba Mandiramdhil Arataya &
Mantrochar - Mp3

Sai Baba Photo Frame

Dateless
Calendar

Divine Gurus

Guru Charitra
Shree Swami Samarth
ISBN 978 81 207 3348 0
₹ 200

**Sri Swami Samarth
Maharaj of Akkalkot**
N.S. Karandikar
ISBN 978 81 207 3445 6
₹ 200

**Hazrat Babajan:
A Pathan Sufi of Poona**
Kevin R. D. Shepherd
ISBN 978 81 207 8698 1
₹ 200

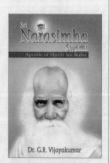

**Sri Narasimha Swami
Apostle of Shirdi Sai Baba**
Dr. G.R. Vijayakumar
ISBN 978 81 207 4432 5
₹ 90

श्री शिरडी साई बाबा

जेल में साई साक्षात्कार
राकेश जुनेजा
978 81 207 9063 6
₹ 150

श्री साई चरित्र दर्शन
मोहन जगन्नाथ यादव
978 81 207 8350 8
₹ 200

श्री साई सच्चरित्र
श्री शिरडी साई बाबा की अद्भुत
जीवनी तथा उनके अमूल्य उपदेश
गोविंद रघुनाथ दाभोलकर (हेमाडपंत)
978 81 207 2501 0   ₹ 250 (PB)
978 81 207 2500 3   ₹ 300 (HB)

शिरडी अंतः से अनंत
डॉ. रबिन्द्रनाथ ककरिया
978 81 207 8191 7
₹ 750

साई सुमिरन
अंजु टंडन
978 81 207 8706 3
₹ 90

**बाबा की वाणी-उनके
वचन तथा आदेश**
बेला शर्मा
978 81 207 4745 6
₹ 100

बाबा का अनुराग
विनी चितलूरी
978 81 207 6699 0
₹ 100

बाबा का ऋणानुबंध
विनी चितलूरी
978 81 207 5998 5
₹ 150

बाबा का गुरूकुल-शिरडी
विनी चितलूरी
978 81 207 6698 3
₹ 125

साई की आत्मकथा
विकास कपूर
978 81 207 7719 4
₹ 200

बाबा-आध्यात्मिक विचार
चन्द्रभानु सतपथी
978 81 207 4627 5
₹ 150

**पृथ्वी पर अवतरित
भगवान शिरडी के साई बाबा**
रंगास्वामी पार्थसारथी
978 81 207 2101 2
₹ 150

स्टर्लिंग

श्री शिरडी साई बाबा एवं अन्य सद्गुरु
चन्द्रभानु सतपथी
978 81 207 4401 1
₹ 90

साई शरण में
चन्द्रभानु सतपथी
978 81 207 2802 8
₹ 150

साई - सबका मालिक
कल्पना भाकुनी
978 81 207 3320 6
₹ 125

साई बाबा एक अवतार
बेला शर्मा
978 81 207 6706 5
₹ 100

साई सत् चरित का प्रकाश
बेला शर्मा
978 81 207 7804 7
₹ 200

श्री साई बाबा के परम भक्त
डॉ. रबिन्द्रनाथ ककरिया
978 81 207 2779 3
₹ 75

श्री साई बाबा के उपदेश व तत्त्वज्ञान
लेफ्टिनेंट कर्नल
एम. बी. निंबालकर
978 81 207 5971 8   ₹ 100

साई भक्तानुभव
डॉ. रबिन्द्रनाथ ककरिया
978 81 207 3052 6
₹ 125

श्री साई बाबा के अनन्य भक्त
डॉ. रबिन्द्र नाथ ककरिया
978 81 207 2705 2
₹ 100

साई का संदेश
डॉ. रबिन्द्र नाथ ककरिया
978 81 207 2879 0
₹ 125

शिरडी संपूर्ण दर्शन
डॉ. रबिन्द्रनाथ ककरिया
978 81 207 2312 2
₹ 50

मुक्तिदाता - श्री साई बाबा
डॉ. रबिन्द्रनाथ ककरिया
978 81 207 2778 6
₹ 65

साई दत्तावधूता
राजेन्द्र भण्डारी
978 81 207 4400 4
₹ 75

साई हरि कथा
दासगणु महाराज
978 81 207 3323 7
₹ 65

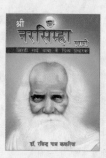

श्री नरसिम्हा स्वामी
शिरडी साई बाबा के
दिव्य प्रचारक
डॉ. रबिन्द्र नाथ ककरिया
978 81 207 4437 0   ₹ 75

शिरडी साई बाबा - की सत्य कथाओं से प्राप्त - एक पावन प्रतिज्ञा
प्रो. डॉ. बी.एच. ब्रिज-किशोर
978 81 207 2346 7   ₹ 80

शिरडी साई बाबा की दिव्य लीलाएँ
डॉ. रबिन्द्र नाथ ककरिया
978 81 207 6376 0   ₹ 150

श्री साई चालीसा
978 81 207 4773 9
₹ 50

शिरडी साई बाबा आरती
978 81 207 8195 5
₹ 10

आरती संग्रह (Boardbook)
ISBN 978 81 207 9057 5
Size: 10.70 cm x 15.45 cm
₹ 100

शिरडी साई के दिव्य वचन-सब का मालिक एक
प्रतिदिन का विचार
978 81 207 3533 0
₹ 180

Oriya Language

శ్రీ సాఇ సఙచరిత (Oriya)
శ్రీ గోఇందరావ రఘునాథ దాఖొలకర
(హేమడపంత)
978 81 207 8332 4 ₹ 300

శ్రీ శిరిడి సాఇబాబా కథామృత
ప్రఫెసర ఇ. బి. ఎన్. త్రిజికిశొర (Oriya)
978 81 207 7774 3
₹ 80

శిరుడి సాఇ బాబాఙ జీవన చరిత (Oriya)
అమూల శాయ్సీఇబ రాఉ
అనువాదక - కిశొర చంద్ర పటనాయక
978 81 207 7417 9 ₹ 125

Other Indian Languages

శిరుడిసాయిబాబా (Telugu)
ప్రో. డా. బి.ఎచ. బ్రిజ–కిశొర
978 81 207 2294 1
₹ 80

శ్రీశిరిడి సాయిబాబా ఛరిత (Kannada)
ప్రో. డా. బి.ఎచ. బ్రిజ–కిశొర
978 81 207 2873 8
₹ 80

శ్రీశిరడి సాయిబాబావిన (Tamil)
ఉణ్మైమక్కతైకళిలిరుందు పెరుమైమిమాన వాక్కుప్పుఘ
ప్రో. డా. బి.ఎచ. బ్రిజ–కిశొర
978 81 207 2876 9
₹ 80

శ్రీ శిరడి సాయిబాబావిన దివ్య ఉపదేశ్
978 81 207 8930 2
₹225

Shirdi Sai Baba Aratis
(Tamil) ₹ 10

Shirdi Sai Baba Aratis
(Telugu) ₹ 10

Shirdi Sai Baba Aratis
(Kannada) ₹ 10

शिरडी साईबाबांची दिव्य वचने (Marathi)
सबका मालिक एक
दैनंदिन विचार
978 81 207 7518 3 ₹ 180

STERLING PUBLISHERS PVT. LTD.

Regd. Office: A-59, Okhla Industrial Area, Phase-II, New Delhi-110020, CIN: U22110PB1964PTC002569
For Online order & detailed Catalogue visit our website:
www.sterlingpublishers.com, E-mail : mail@sterlingpublishers.com, Tel. 91-11-26386165, 26387070